To Colin, Ian and James

Commissioning Editor Stuart Cooper
Editor Helen Woodhall
Editorial Assistant Maxine McCaghy
Copy Editor Sharon Amos

Designer Amanda Lerwill
Picture Research Julia Pashley and Mel Watson

Production Amanda Sneddon
Index Helen Snaith

First published in 1998 by
Conran Octopus Limited
37 Shelton Street
London WC2H 9HN

ISBN 1 85029 994 3

British Library Cataloguing-in-Publication Data
A catalogue record for this book is available from the British Library.

Printed and bound in China

previous page Columbines (*Aquilegia*), corn cockle (the annual *Agrostemma
githago*) and toadflax (*Linaria maroccana*) make a quick and easy combination
for cottage gardens.
left Variegated flag iris (*Iris pseudacorus*) and *Primula pulverulenta* are an
effective combination for a late nineteenth-century planting in a damp border.
far right Tagetes, popular since the seventeenth century, form pretty rows
amongst onions, and may even keep pests at bay.
overleaf Borage (*Borago officinalis*) and marigolds (*Calendula officinalis*) have
been a classic combination since at least medieval times.

classic plant
combinations

David Stuart

conran
OCTOPUS

contents

Introduction

A classic plant combination is created when the flowers or foliage, or both, of each species involved make an impact that is greater than the sum of its parts, and which has a beauty that withstands changes in fashion.

That such a fortuitous combination is possible has been appreciated in garden cultures since earliest times, and in recent years some gardeners and designers have become renowned for their ability to combine garden plants in ways that become instant classics. Some are famous for a single garden, often their own; others for a whole range of commissions.

There can be no doubt that the ancient Egyptians appreciated the juxtaposition of plant form and colour, for the frescos in many tombs show delightfully elegant and productive gardens, designed to give pleasure and sustenance both to the living and to the spirits of the dead. The ancient sacred lotus (*Nelumbo nucifera*), which provided edible tubers as well as being rich in religious symbolism, is often beautifully paired with the papyrus plant (*Cyperus papyrus*) in water scenes, and fruit and flower gardens are shown fringed with decorative margins of stylized date palms and olives.

Roman frescos, especially in some of the grand houses of Rome and Pompeii, depict gardens filled with birds and other game, the trees laden with fruit and lilies heavy with flowers. Pomegranates and red cabbage roses

far left above A Japanese Kano school screen of the late 1700s, showing a battered and contorted plum tree still cheerfully flowering, against a tall bamboo whose evergreen foliage symbolizes constancy and vigour in old age.

far left below Gardens in ancient Egypt combined rows of silvery, gnarled olive trees with the graceful, dark green glitter of palm foliage. This is the garden of Ialu, from the Sennudem tomb at Thebes, c. 1200BC.

above Ducks rise from alternate clumps of stylized papyrus and lotus in this painted decoration from the palace of Amenhotep at Malqata, now in the Egyptian Museum, Cairo.

right A Roman fresco from around the first century AD shows an orchard planting at the Empress Livia's house at Prima Porta, Italy. Red multi-petalled roses flourish beneath pomegranates and are combined with ox-eye daisies and cypress trees. It would still make a splendid planting today, suitable for all but the coldest of gardens.

are commonly pictured together; the combination is probably symbolic, for the pomegranate represented marital bliss and fecundity, while the rose, beautiful but thorned, gave a different message. Many of these frescos illustrated a supposed Golden Age of gardens, and some ideas were taken from older Greek models. For example, the ancient Greeks believed pomegranates were brought by the gods to Greece from the Elysian fields.

In the Middle and Far East, too, plant combinations often took on symbolic meanings: in ancient Persia, the weeping willow was a symbol of Majnun, the lover of the drowned Laila, in turn symbolized by the water lily; and jasmine was a symbol of Vohuman, the archangel of good spirits and divine wisdom in Zoroastrian thinking, as well as of woman's loveliness. It was commonly entwined with roses and honeysuckle.

Though little is known about gardening in Europe after the fall of Rome, the so-called Dark Ages were turbulent times, particularly in Eastern and Southern Europe, and may have seen at least some traffic in garden plants and ideas, most notably from the sumptuous Asian splendours of Byzantium. However, a number of new introductions (*Lychnis chalcedonica*, for instance), were, at least in legend, associated with the various Crusades, and certainly enough barbarian Crusaders fell in love with Byzantine and Moorish gardens to build themselves copies in places as far apart as Hesdin in northern France and Palermo in Sicily, suggesting that the European gardens of the time were not captivating places.

The later medieval period is much richer in information about how plants were grown together and a few plant combinations exist from this time such as Madonna Lily (*Lilium candidum*), *Iris germanica* and columbine (*Aquilegia vulgaris*), an association found in many religious paintings.

In the distant Orient, a comprehensive and decorative record of plant combinations can be found in the paintings on screens, scrolls and ceramics from around 800AD. These early works of art soon established such a powerful

below left This Roman mosaic, from Tunisia, shows young vines grown in pots twining around the upright stems of millet which has been sown in the same pot. The method of cultivation is comparable to the central American use of maize and climbing squashes (see page 70).

below right Though this fifteenth-century tapestry of the Lady and the Unicorn is an allegory of smell, the richly detailed background shows a pretty fenced-off garden, with a sophisticated meadow combination of violets, columbines and wild strawberries woven into the grass. Other late-medieval combinations can be recreated with honesty, sweet rocket, and the lovely thistle *Silybum marianum*.

above A handpainted wallpaper of about 1760 from the Chateau de Maintenon, France, showing a stylized pink-flowered prunus, perhaps a peach, teamed with a bamboo. Whether the paper was painted in China (as many similar papers were) or in Europe, it shows how long lived ancient combinations can be, and how widespread their appreciation. In the garden, a pruned peach tree in a large container looks splendid in front of a screen of bamboo such as *Phyllostachys nigra*.

influence on taste that the traditional combinations have lasted into modern times: paintings of the nineteenth century often show the sort of plant combinations that were considered perfection a thousand years before.

Arabic influences are much harder to judge and come mostly from literary material. Islam forbids the depiction of anything but the most stylized plant forms, and although carpets, fabrics, mosaic work and paintings show what could be a dianthus or a tulip, or willows and cypress, few other planting ideas can be gleaned – even though Arab rulers were known to be passionate gardeners and collectors of plants.

It is only in Renaissance Europe, and with the widespread use of letterpress and woodcut printing, that the first substantial body of planting combinations can be discovered. Not surprisingly, most of these have long ceased to be

credited to one specific gardener and have, instead, become part of the traditional plantings of the garden. They have survived in contemporary writings, particularly in the many garden books that date from the sixteenth and early seventeenth century, in turn culled from prestigious works like John Gerard's *Herball*, and, more particularly, John Parkinson's *Paradisi in Sole Paradisus Terrestris* of 1629 or John Rea's *A Complete Florilege* (1655).

Paintings of the time show gardens only rarely, and often simply as a background to a portrait of a grandee. In any case, most gardening then and even in the eighteenth century was inspired by the impulse to collect rather than to beautify: gardeners were more concerned to have enormous, or at least interesting, ranges of different flowers and shrubs. Though some information exists on how plants were arranged in beds, it seems they were

left The combination depicted on this scroll can be recreated by underplanting double decorative cherries with paeonies and irises such as *Iris japonica* and *I. ensata*.
right Albrecht Dürer's painting of 1503 was the first in Europe to look objectively at something as simple as a clod of earth. This intensity of observation developed into scientific botany, and into the combination of plants for purely decorative reasons.

combined in mathematically based ways in carefully laid out grids, rather than in visually satisfying combinations.

The great age in Europe, really the beginning of planting design, started with the craze for bedding gardens from 1820 or so. There were many reasons for its rise – political, economic and botanical – but the end result was the same: huge numbers of new plants had been arriving in Western Europe since the second half of the eighteenth century, especially half-hardy species from central America, South Africa and tropical Asia. These include important groups like verbenas, pelargoniums, calceolarias, salvias, penstemons and many more. None of them could easily be fitted into the standard landscape garden which was then fashionable, and though some gardens had areas devoted to flowering plants, the over-riding passion of garden theorists and designers was really landscape, not flowers.

In about 1820 or so, a few English garden owners decided to cut beds into their extensive lawns and fill them with some of the new flowers. This apparently inconsequential step unleashed a huge flood of excitement, not least because it at last enabled those with tiny plots to copy what grand gardeners were doing.

The ensuing revolt against landscape gardening and the search for a style which was possible in middle-class or prosperous working-class gardens coincided with improvements in printing text and pictures. New garden books and magazines – filled with planting plans and interesting plant combinations – fuelled excitement about the new freedoms. For the first time, with so much documentary evidence, classic plantings can often be attributed to a single designer, so your own garden today can feature plantings by Sir Joseph Paxton (1801–65) or any other of the great mid-nineteenth century designers.

The bedding craze began to decline in the late nineteenth century under the withering attack of gardeners like William Robinson (1838–1935), whose book *The Wild Garden,* published in 1870, advocated a move towards a more natural style of gardening in which the gardener should take nature as his example in the approach to garden design.

The herbaceous garden grew in popularity, producing many great designers and plantsmen and women. The influence of Gertrude Jekyll (1843–1932), was especially important: using her training as an artist, she made painterly colour combinations, and often employed changing sequences of colour through the length of a border – and sometimes through the seasons, too.

Though perhaps her most famous garden was the one she created around her own house at Munstead Wood in Surrey, England, she designed many others. Her gardens throughout the UK and especially at Barrington Court, Hestercombe and Lindisfarne are now being restored, but even in the short time between creation and restoration, many of the plant varieties she used have vanished. Luckily, plenty of her schemes and their derivatives were

above This turn-of-the-century herbaceous
planting, painted by George Samuel Elgood
(1851–1943), includes *Anthemis tinctoria* 'E. C.
Buxton', annual bread-seed poppies and larkspurs
or small delphiniums. The soft yellow of the
anthemis sets off the silvery-blue larkspurs.
right Jean Monet's 'Lady in the Garden' shows a
meadow-like planting amongst wild and unpruned
shrubs. The scene could be recreated by sowing
grasses with corn cockle, cosmos, nigella and
Shirley poppies, and using large philadelphus
varieties and double lilacs for the shrub backing.

captured in photographs or in the paintings of Anna Leigh Merritt and Edith
A. Andrews, both of whom produced huge numbers of sentimentalized
pictures of Jekyll's new style of planting.

Great late nineteenth-century painters, too, were inspired by their own or
their friends' gardens and captured, if in impressionistic ways, not only the
changes in style of garden design in the last decades of the nineteenth
century, but also the look of individual plantings. A number of artists were
also gardeners. Renoir's garden still has huge plantings of the pale blue iris
'Aline', named after his wife; and Monet's garden at Giverny in northern
France, first photographed in the 1920s, notably by *Country Life*, is still
enormously influential on today's plantings.

When Monet started gardening, Europeans were discovering the art of
Japan, and rediscovering that of China. Fans, screens, ceramics and brocade
from the East were in every fashionable Western drawing room. At the same

time bamboos, maples and stone lanterns appeared in gardens, as did bridges like the one at Giverny, draped with wisteria and spanning ponds stocked with new varieties of water lily, which were bred in the West from varieties grown for centuries in the East.

Only a few decades separate gardeners in Monet's time from great planting designers of the mid-twentieth century like Vita Sackville-West, and only one or two more from contemporary designers such as Roberto Burle Marx, James van Sweden, Wolfgang Oehme and Piet Oudolf.

Vita Sackville-West's garden at Sissinghurst Castle in Kent has become a source of innumerable classic combinations, typified by her use of the colour pink in combining tamarisk (*Tamarix ramosissima*) with pink aquilegias as a starting point, and extending the combination with the sharp pink of the perfumed rose 'Ispahan' and a bearded iris called 'Senlac'. Roberto Burle Marx worked almost entirely with tropical plants, and used their architectural qualities in masterly ways, mixing *Vriesia imperialis* and *Philodendron bipinnatifidum*, or planting *Agave werklei* in a sea of purple-leaved setcreasea, as he did at the Bank of Brazil in Brasilia.

The American James van Sweden is noted for his imaginative use of North American flora, whether he is combining woodland plantings in a way that mirrors the natural structure of woods, or rich grassland flora to create prairie gardens. The Dutchman Piet Oudolf is more eclectic in his choice of plants, using many new varieties produced by European hybridizers.

Throughout this book, the plantings are grouped into garden areas and types, with plantings ranging from the gardens of ancient Greece and Rome, through the gardens of Mughal emperors, to the traditional plantings of the great herbaceous borders of late Victorian and Edwardian England and, lastly, to modern plantings worldwide, from Brussels to New York. These last are, for the most part, attributed to a particular gardener or garden designer, and where they are not, the plantings have been selected on the basis of their popularity or fashionable status among contemporary gardeners.

above If the garden architecture is good, as here in George Elgood's painting of a yew arbour by an apple tree, then a simple combination of annuals makes an effective contrast. Here, *Papaver somniferum* 'Pink Chiffon' and a single form called 'Danish Flag' (which has a white base to the petals) work well against the darker background planting.

below right This wonderful painting by Vincent van Gogh, of lilac and irises, can easily be recreated in the garden. For the lilac, use either *Syringa x persica*, or a hybrid like 'Marie Legraye' (whose small but emphatic flower trusses can be seen in many gardens in the south of France, and is possibly the one depicted by van Gogh here), or 'Maud Notcutt'. Add some blue-black irises such as 'Sable Night' or 'Swazi Princess'. Finish off with forms of *Anthemis tinctoria* along with a sparse scatter of scarlet potentillas.

The plantings range from those suitable for walls and pergolas, woodland and pondside, to others suitable for wildflower meadows, or kitchen and cottage gardens, sophisticated herbaceous borders or collectors' gardens. They include combinations that will be glorious in early spring through to those that will make autumn splendid; many will still be worth looking at in deepest winter. Some will do best in shade, others in full sun; some will grow perfectly in cold gardens, a few others need warmth and shelter. All have been selected not only for their beauty, but also for the ease with which any gardener can grow the plants and for simplicity of maintenance.

For each entry there is also advice on how to augment the basic combinations so that the plantings can have even greater richness or length of season; the suggestions are taken from other species used by the original designer, or ones that I have used myself in similar combinations. Sometimes, too, the combinations are linked to others with which they make especially good associations. As well as information on how to propagate and maintain both plants and plantings, you will also find guidance (in the List of Suppliers

on page 155) on where to buy the plants. The book concludes with a listing of gardens in both the UK and farther afield to visit where classic combinations, either recreated or in their original situations, can be seen.

Each chapter profiles a famous planting designer. With so many outstanding gardeners to choose from, this involved many difficult decisions. In the end, we chose designers who have developed one recent strand of planting design, even if their creative imagination has been focused on only one garden. After all, nowadays, a single garden that captures the eye of writers and photographers can easily win as much influence for its creator as could 50 major commissions.

However, even where the original designer of a classic plant combination is quite unknown, the plants still have a history that gives their beauty an extra and, I hope, fascinating significance.

above 'A Pathway in Monet's garden, Giverny', painted by the artist in 1902, shows the famous arches and walk in late afternoon towards the end of summer. The borders were probably made of asters (maybe newly introduced hybrids of *Aster novi-belgii*) and Japanese anemones in shades of deep pink and white, with trimmed mats of nasturtiums at their base.

Climbers
and
Wall Plants

above An old wall of grey stone is softened by generous swags of a white climbing rose, underplanted with campanulas and pink and white valerians to make a luxurious garden view. A shady wall like this could also support any sort of clematis, honeysuckle or ivy.

right The range of garden climbers is huge, but here a high wall looks splendid with the easiest and most rampant of all – *Clematis montana*. Some forms of this species have an alluring perfume too. Walls also provide warmth and shelter, so can be used to support exotics like vines, tender jasmines, and bignonias in climates colder than they normally tolerate. Here, *Macleaya cordata* will fill one of the beds by high summer.

CLIMBERS HAVE ALWAYS BEEN USED IN GARDENS, especially to give shade to domestic buildings. First seen in the palace courtyards of Mesopotamia, simple pergolas and vine arbours were common in ancient Greece, and were widespread in all classes of Roman gardens. Some plant combinations that were used by the ancient Romans are still in use, for example grape vines growing over the branches of the 'Peche de Vigne' peach, a Roman variety which is still available in southern France.

In Europe, pergolas were adapted over the centuries, and by the sixteenth century they had become trellis arcades and pavilions, recorded in many contemporary illustrations. In some gardens – as at Zorgvliet, William of Orange's palace in Holland – obelisks of trellis were used to support climbers. This device is still used in many contemporary gardens to great effect, as long as the vigour of the plant is matched carefully to its support.

Though the Americas had a much richer flora of climbers and lianas – climbers of tropical origins – only climbing beans seem to have been used with any degree of frequency. The old kitchen garden combination of squashes, sweetcorn and beans is quite probably pre-Columbian in origin.

Climbers have not always been used simply to give shade: walls, pergolas and screens have long been utilized as places to display plants. In ancient China and Japan, gardeners built pergolas just to show their wisterias to perfection. Similarly in nineteenth-century Europe, when rose breeding began in earnest, pergolas and other structures were used to show off the thousands of new hybrid climbing roses.

Great designers have always been attracted to climbers. Humphry Repton often used rose-covered trellis arches, and later Gertrude Jekyll trained grand roses along ropes slung between arches in the loggia of her house at Munstead Wood. William Robinson did similar things at Gravetye Manor in Kent, while in America bignonia and its relatives twined round the arbours of many nineteenth-century gardens – particularly those in Pennsylvania.

above Ivy growing up a wall or high fence can be combined with clipped holly bushes (standards are traditional) planted immediately in front. Nothing looks better than the subtle foliage of plain ivy and glossy leaves of plain holly, but variegated holly can clash badly with variegated ivy.

right Roses and honeysuckle make a fine combination; in ancient gardens, the old cream double musk rose would have been used. To recreate this planting, use *R.* 'Russelliana', a Spanish hybrid from the 1840s. The honeysuckle is the pale native form of *Lonicera periclymenum*; the cultivar 'Graham Thomas' is a good alternative.

Ancient

Most early plant combinations were first used in enclosed spaces: the atria of Roman houses, cloisters of medieval monasteries, or the walled courtyards of seventeenth-century noblemen where they gave shade, perfume or fruit. Today they are at home in shaded backyards, or in sunny ones, where they can give privacy and a cool spot to sit when thrown over pergolas or arbours to make leafy pavilions.

roses and honeysuckle

Roses (*Rosa*) and honeysuckle (*Lonicera*) have been a favourite combination twined around a doorway or window since ancient times, and could be found in both Greek and Roman gardens. The rounded fullness of the rose makes a satisfying contrast with the honeysuckle's clusters of narrow trumpets, whose perfume is strongest in the evening as that of the rose diminishes.

In ancient European gardens, climbing roses were few, though the full creamy-white *Rosa* x *alba* 'Alba Maxima' could reach 3m (10ft) and more. Sixteenth-century gardens were filled with the old perfumed musk rose (*R. moschata*) in single and double forms. The creamy flowers make a perfect foil to the buff and pale yellow flowers of the ordinary hedgerow honeysuckle, or to the more powerfully coloured 'Belgica' and 'Serotina'. The musk rose does best in warm gardens; in northern ones try its hybrids, such as the vigorous 'Paul's Himalayan Musk', or the enchanting 'The Garland', both with pale pinkish-amethyst flowers. Either rose, tangled with honeysuckle, will eventually produce huge, heavy volumes of vegetation, so they should be securely anchored to the wall or fence you plan to cover.

Although it lacks a perfume, the flowers of *Lonicera sempervirens* are an intense coral red which looks good with *Rosa* 'Rambling Rector', or even pink 'Aloha'. For a late-summer combination, with *R.* 'Blush Noisette' or 'New Dawn', try the almost evergreen *L. japonica* 'Halliana' – its flowers, though not showy, smell wonderful.

cultivation Both plants like fertile, well-drained soil. Many of the roses suitable for this combination like full sun, though most of the honeysuckles will cheerfully flower in shade. If your garden is shady, plant *Rosa* 'Mme. Alfred Carrière' which flowers reasonably well on a north-facing wall. Remove old stems from the base every few years.
extending the grouping *Jasminum officinale* is a natural addition for gardens in mild areas, but for flowers early in the season try a clematis, such as pale blue 'Columbine', a form of *Clematis alpina*.

holly and ivy

Holly (*Ilex*) and ivy (*Hedera*) have been combined in northern gardens since pre-Roman times. Poet's ivy (*H. helix poetarum*) is a yellow-berried ivy that was grown by the Romans and is still available today. Variants of holly, mostly with variegated leaves, were available by the seventeenth century, so some antique combinations are easily made.

Both holly and ivy thrive in shade and so make excellent formal (and evergreen) plantings in tiny urban gardens or front yards. Of ivy variants, try the grand, deep green *Hedera helix* 'Bowles Ox Heart', or the variegated 'Tricolor'. Some sorts (such as *H. helix* 'Buttercup') have all-yellow leaves, a colour that can be intimidating in large areas. Of hollies, many of the yellow-or white- variegated sorts (such as *I.* x *altaclerensis* 'Golden King') look best and are traditionally grown as topiaries, but remember that you will not get berries this way.

cultivation Both plants prefer well-drained soil. The ivy varieties given above are good climbers, but not all types are, so check the variety before you plant. To prune hollies, use secateurs rather than shears, which can cause damage to the leaves. Topiary hollies need clipping twice during the growing season. Use ivy as a ground cover beneath the holly, against a wall, or as a topiary in its own right.
extending the grouping Add tough ferns like *Dryopteris* and *Athyrium*, winter- and spring-flowering hellebores, and, if the garden gets some sunshine, single or double bloodroot (*Sanguinaria canadensis*). For summer flowers, plant up big pots with white datura.

The range of climbing flora in Europe was quite sparse until the late eighteenth century and was confined to musk roses, honeysuckles, jasmines and a few clematis. Even in North America where the native climbing flora is very much richer, there were hardly more garden climbers than in Europe. With the collapse of the landscape ideal by the early 1800s, everything changed, and pergolas, arbours and poles covered with climbers became essential in even the smallest garden. There was a new era of publishing, too, so these 'new' planting ideas were rapidly disseminated throughout Europe, the settled Americas, and even the Orient, and soon came to be seen as 'traditional'.

roses and clematis

The combination of roses and clematis has always attracted gardeners. The largely simple shapes of the clematis flower, whether flat and star-shaped in some modern hybrids, or elegantly bell-shaped in species like *Clematis texensis* and its offspring, combine perfectly with the more complex form and often opulent texture of the rose. Initially, the combinations available were limited to *Rosa moschata* and *C. viticella*, or possibly *R. x alba* 'Alba Maxima' and *C. flammula*. However, by the beginning of the nineteenth century some huge clambering roses and several new clematis species had reached European gardens from America and China.

Species of clematis can be found in flower throughout the rose season and beyond. Some forms of *Clematis montana* catch the first roses while *C. montana* var. *wilsonii* flowers for much of the season, combining well with sprays of *Rosa* 'Awakening'. Numerous hybrid clematis flower in high summer, so choice is not a problem. Later in the year, *C. viticella* has some lovely forms, including deep purple doubles that are a foil for *R.* 'Golden Showers'. Try also *C. rehderiana*, with its clusters of tubular cream flowers smelling of primroses, amongst *R.* 'Constance Spry'.

cultivation Most clematis are hardy but some climbing roses will not survive the toughest winters. Both genera will grow in ordinary garden soils, and most species like full sun though you should aim to keep the roots of clematis in shade, particularly when the plants are young. Both plants must be pruned annually otherwise an impenetrable tangle will result. Early-flowering clematis cannot be cut back until after flowering, by which time you should avoid disturbing the rose – this can be tricky.

extending the grouping Pale-coloured honeysuckles work well with nearly any rose and clematis combination but steer clear of most jasmines, which are too vigorous and swamp the main planting. Best of all are the ornamental vines: I've used *Clematis* x *jouiniana* and *Rosa* 'Félicité Perpétue' mixed with vines like the purple-leaved *Vitis* 'Brant', which turns scarlet in autumn, and silver *Vinifera* 'Incana'.

far left *Clematis* 'Venosa Violacea' is a vigorous and late-flowering variety that complements the second flush of lightly scented flowers from *Rosa* 'Karlsruhe'. The clematis has upward-facing flowers so plant it where you can view them from above.

above The moderately vigourous *Clematis* 'Elsa Späth' which flowers from late spring until autumn, combines well with the shrubby habit of old roses, including 'Mme. Isaac Pereire', as shown here.

overleaf left to right *Rosa* 'American Pillar' and *Clematis* 'Jackmanii'; *R.* 'Iceberg' and *C.* 'Henryi', and *R.* 'Paul's Scarlet Climber' and *C.* 'William Kennett' – three sumptuous ways of combining a rose and a clematis.

yew and
tropaeolum

Though yew (*Taxus baccata*) is a very ancient garden plant, the flame flower (*Tropaeolum speciosum*) only reached yew-growing gardens from Chile in 1846. Its perennial rootstock was found to do well in cool dry shade, such as that created by hedges, and as yew hedges are usually pruned early and very late in the season, the swift growth of the climber allowed a dazzling show of brilliant red flowers against dark green foliage during the intervening summer months. Despite its rapid growth rate, the climber never becomes dense enough to starve the yew foliage of light.

The combination works best using large yew hedges, although tropaeolum looks good on topiary, too. Avoid combining it with box (*Buxus*) as the trees, unlike yew, are shallow rooted, and so starve the climber. Fast-growing privet (*Ligustrum*) and lonicera hedges are also unsuitable, as they need summer clipping. Canary creeper (*Tropaeolum peregrinum*), a fast-growing annual, can be used instead of flame flower, and looks especially good growing up golden yew (*T. baccata* Aurea Group).

cultivation The tropaeolum prefers cool gardens that have well-drained soil and it is quite happy in shade. It can sometimes be difficult to establish, so for the best results buy potted plants. Thereafter the new tubers form at least 30cm (1ft) below soil level, making them difficult to dig up and shift, so you will have to let the plant increase at its own pace. If using canary creeper, plant seed about 30cm (1ft) in front of the hedge during spring and train towards the hedge.

extending the grouping Yew hedges can also make good supports for the rampant scarlet-flowered *Phygelius capensis*, while the basic hedge would look good made with several species (see page 50). A combination of yew and beech, especially the purple-foliaged *Fagus sylvatica* Atropurpurea Group would augment the contrast with the flame flower. Few other climbers work as well in this situation, though a hedge in my garden has wild honeysuckle wound through it that survives being clipped as part of the hedge.

above This sumptuous combination of scarlet *Tropaeolum speciosum* and dark green yew has become a traditional combination in Europe and parts of North America. The tropaeolum also looks good scrambling over bushes of *Daphne retusa* and tree paeonies, and through bush roses – it flowers later than most roses. If it likes your garden, it can become somewhat invasive.

left With even a modest amount of feeding, *Tropaeolum speciosum* can be very vigorous, though its foliage is never dense enough to starve its supporting plant of light.

Designer

Eighteenth-century fashion decreed that climber-covered cottages looked 'romantic' – as a result everyone wanted their houses swathed with ivies, roses, clematis and honeysuckle. But climbers were needed on garden walls, pergolas and outbuildings too, and in the following two centuries plantsmen and designers from Humphry Repton to Russell Page and Lanning Roper began to explore the climbing flora of the world. It was an exciting time: species from every continent were exploited – from quick-growing annuals to rampant tropical lianas. The 'Old World' garden flora was ransacked for vines, Oriental garden flora for wisterias, and the New World for bougainvilleas, bignonias, passionflowers and much else. Here are some classics: use them on porches, arbours or an arch over a garden seat.

hostas and hop

This arresting combination is a clever way of unifying upright climbers and the ground planting at their base: strands of golden hop (*Humulus lupulus* 'Aurea') have been allowed to ramble amongst a bold group of blue-leaved hostas first popularized by Gertrude Jekyll.

Both plants do well in partial shade, so this planting suits a small overshadowed space. If the soil is damp, it will combine well with the rodgersias and primulas on page 46; a trellis arbour by a pool can be planted with the hop, the whole rising up from the hostas.

cultivation Golden hop cannot be raised from seed. You need to buy young plants and feed them well for the first season or so. Eventually, the plants might get too vigorous for your garden; keep them under control by thinning the young shoots in spring – they are delicious cooked and eaten like asparagus. Once winter sets in, pull the dead stems away from their support. Wear gloves as the stems are abrasive. Hostas like rich, moist but well-drained soil, and are propagated by division in spring.

extending the grouping Add the big jagged leaves and hot yellow flowers of *Ligularia przewalskii*, and the narrow arching leaves of one of the forms of flag iris (*Iris pseudacorus*) which grow perfectly well in ordinary border soil despite their natural waterside habitat. The variegated form is ideal. Alternatively, add the ordinary green-leaved hop. It is easily grown from seed and will also give you the bonus of trusses of papery fruits. Rosemary Verey uses golden hop on arches amongst deep violet lavender *Lavandula angustifolia* 'Hidcote' and 'White Pet' standard roses. Lawrence Johnston used it at Hidcote as backing to a planting of the yellow tree paeony (a clever foliage combination) and *Thalictrum flavum* ssp. *glaucum*.

clematis and vine

Used on the walls at Vita Sackville-West's garden in Sissinghurst, Kent, and by Gertrude Jekyll on the pergolas at Hestercombe, Somerset, this combination of clematis and vine (*Vitis*) demonstrates how sombre colours can come into their own in the garden. Try *Clematis* 'Perle d'Azur' with the purple-leaved vine (*Vitis vinifera* 'Purpurea'). This is a planting with bags of value: the vine's leaves slowly turn scarlet in autumn, setting off the glaucous black grapes. This makes a perfect planting for a wall, on an arch over a seat, over a porch or along a grand arbour. *V. vinifera* 'Incana' is another interesting vine, often known as the dusty miller grape because of its white mealy leaves. Try it with a big white clematis like 'Henryi' or one of the outrageous double pinkish-lilac ones such as 'Proteus'.

cultivation If you are growing the vine solely to produce grapes, there is a lot of pruning involved; if not, just let it clamber at will and only thin it out when it gets too dense. As the clematis can be left to flower when it likes, do not prune until it, too, becomes tangled.

extending the grouping Try the glitzy foliage of the kiwi fruit (*Actinidia deliciosa* 'Aureovariegata') or the more subtle *A. kolomikta*. Alternatively, add a late-flowering clematis like *C. texensis*, or a hybrid like 'Gravetye Beauty', named after William Robinson's house.

above This hosta, a hybrid of *H. sieboldiana*, will produce pale mauve flowers; 'Krossa Regal', with big green leaves and large white perfumed flowers, is worth planting, too.

left The purple-leaved vine, sometimes called the claret vine, does best in full sun. It grows as vigorously as the clematis, so the two are well matched. The vine will flower and fruit when summers are long, and the flowers have a slight fragrance that is delicious.

blackberries and parthenocissus

Some plant combinations, such as the contemporary classic pairing of blackberry (*Rubus fruticosus* cultivars) and *Parthenocissus henryana* are just so good that they shout 'Copy me!' to every passing gardener. In spring, there are blackberry flowers and the pinkish-green foliage of the vine; in autumn, the juxtaposition of the scarlet leaves of the vine and the glossy purple-black of the berries, and the contrast in shape between the vine leaves and clusters of berries.

cultivation Both plants are easily grown in sun or partial shade in well-drained soil. The blackberry needs to be tied in or supported along wires. Thin the vine occasionally to prevent it swamping the berry, and prune old berry canes at ground level after fruiting.

extending the grouping Adding other climbers makes upkeep difficult, but the combination can be extended at ground level: clumps of glossy hellebores and *Iris foetidissima,* with its orange seedpods in autumn, complement both climbers.

cobaea and ipomoea

The sultry green and purple of *Cobaea scandens* (the cup-and saucer-vine) contrasts with the cream and coral firecrackers of *Ipomoea lobata*. They provide quick-growing cover up a sunny wall, and in cold areas an ideal 'instant' planting for a new conservatory, though neither is perfumed and they will need to be sprayed regularly.

cultivation Both are fast-growing annuals – perennial in subtropical gardens – and like full sun and moist, rich soil. In cool gardens, start them off indoors: sow one seed per pot and leave to germinate on a sunny windowsill. Do not plant out until after the last frosts.

extending the grouping In warm gardens, add the dramatic oval leaves of aristolochia, with its strange curved flowers, or the wild exuberance of *Ipomoea tricolor* 'Heavenly Blue'.

above The combination of blackberry and parthenocissus works well over a trellis arbour or pergola and in a kitchen garden or orchard. If growing on a lightly shaded wall, hellebores can be planted beneath to complement the pairing.

far right A luxuriant planting like this can be produced from seed, in good conditions, by high summer: space seedlings at least 45cm (18in) apart, and water and feed generously. The stems can be substantial by the time the first frosts come, so let them dry, then cut into sections using secateurs and carefully untwine from the support.

above *Rosa* 'Mme. Alfred Carrière' embraces an oak tree. Many roses, particularly species like *R. multiflora* and *R. filipes,* are almost as vigorous as tropical lianas. Most of them are nineteenth-century introductions, and there are some delightful modern hybrids

right These laburnums are trained on a framework that makes a substantial tunnel, but the planting would look just as good around a single unpruned tree, or perhaps a group of them.

roses in trees

The practice of growing roses into the branches of old trees was first publicized by William Robinson, who grew *Rosa moschata* up ancient catalpas in his garden at Gravetye, Kent; the combination was then popularized by Vita Sackville-West, who grew 'Rambling Rector' and 'Bobbie James' in her orchard trees at Sissinghurst, Kent. Despite the drawbacks of the combination – growing roses into the branches of fruit trees may damage them, and will make harvesting ripe fruit tricky – it has become a popular one.

Any reasonably sized tree in any garden can be used. Fruit trees are especially suitable because they flower in spring, and the roses start to flower as the fruits begin to form. However, any sort of tree will do, and at the garden of Ninfa in northern Italy, vigorous roses like *R. filipes* 'Kiftsgate' clamber into ancient cypress trees that must have been planted long before the medieval village became a ruin.

Big trees can support any of the roses mentioned above plus 'Seagull' or 'Wedding Day'. These have mostly white or cream flowers; for amethyst-pink plant 'The Garland' (a favourite of Gertrude Jekyll) or 'Paul's Himalayan Musk'. A medium-sized tree will do better with the enchanting and long-flowering 'Blush Noisette'.

cultivation Do not plant the rose too close to the trunk of the tree; leave at least 2m (6ft) between them otherwise their roots will compete for space. Plant the young rose in rich soil in a sunny situation and water it generously in the first season. To encourage the rose into the tree, direct the new growth along a pole leaning on to one of the lower branches. This planting has to use an old, established tree: a young tree will quickly become swamped. Both rose and tree will give you many years of pleasure but eventually a chainsaw will be needed to clear the tangle.

extending the grouping Add clematis: Vita Sackville-West liked 'Hagley Hybrid', but early-flowering sorts can be excellent too. Pale blue *Clematis alpina* 'Columbine' looks exquisite amongst apple branches in blossom, and for colour late in the season plant one of the vine's relatives, like *Parthenocissus henryana*.

laburnum and alliums

Rosemary Verey's famous garden at Barnsley House near Cirencester in Gloucestershire is the source of this combination, where laburnums are grown on a frame to make a tunnel of yellow bloom, softly contrasted with the grey-purple *Allium giganteum* planted beneath. With wild valerian (*Centranthus ruber*), *Lilium regale* and domes of clipped box they make a near-perfect grouping.

It does not have to be a grand tunnel; the idea works perfectly well with a standard laburnum or two – the most floriferous form is *Laburnum* x *watereri* 'Vossii', though *L. alpinum* has the strongest perfume. In a tiny garden, a group of four left as multi-stemmed trees rather than single-stemmed standards could be used to make a screen around a small seating area.

Laburnum seed is poisonous, although a hybrid like *Laburnum* x *watereri* 'Vossii' is sterile, and so produces no seed. There are many garden plants far more dangerous, but if you don't want laburnums, the golden rain tree (*Koelreuteria paniculata*) could be substituted in a mild area. In a sheltered garden, try mimosas; the purple tones could be sharpened up with *Gladiolus* species like *G. byzantinus*, and kept going right into autumn with *Nerine bowdenii*. You could even reverse the colour scheme entirely, growing purple-flowered wisteria underplanted with yellow *Allium flavum* and pale yellow roses.

cultivation Alliums and laburnums both like sun and fertile soil, and all varieties except *Laburnum* x *watereri* 'Vossii' can be easily grown from seed. If you are growing them on a framework, tie in new shoots in late summer, and, in well-established tunnels, take out the oldest wood at the same time. Buy the alliums as bulbs and thereafter they will sow themselves.

extending the grouping The laburnum has a short flowering season; adding a white clematis will give you blooms later in the summer, while filling the borders with euphorbias and phloxes will deal with spring and late summer respectively. Clumps of Japanese anemones and small-flowered aster hybrids (like *Aster cordifolius* 'Silver Spray') will extend the interest into late autumn.

Gertrude Jekyll

right The pergola at Hestercombe, Somerset, a superbly restored garden which shows Jekyll at her best. Palest amethyst and coral-red roses scramble up the pillars, which are underplanted with broad beds of 'Old English' lavender.

BORN INTO A PROSPEROUS MIDDLE-CLASS FAMILY, GERTRUDE JEKYLL (1843–1932), studied as an artist-craftswoman at London's South Kensington School of Art. Her talents meant she was soon working for a varied and influential clientele. During one of her commissions, she met gardener-turned-publisher William Robinson, and was profoundly influenced by his ideas about gardening. Her first major garden was at her family home, Munstead, in Surrey. It was a great success and visitors were soon asking her to advise on their own gardens. She designed more than three hundred gardens, some very grand, but many to suit houses of moderate size, with perhaps an acre or two of land.

Her use of climbers was often particularly imaginative, whether it involved using one of her favourite roses, 'The Garland', slung from ropes linking the loggia pillars in her own house at Munstead Wood, or putting together a striking combination of purple-leaved vines and clematis on the pergolas of a great house like Hestercombe in Somerset. Her own garden featured Banksian roses combined with *Solanum crispum*, and aristolochias, with their great heart-shaped leaves, delicately entwined with wisteria and Virginia creepers.

In the flower borders, she used the very latest hybrids from European nurseries, concentrating in particular on asters, lupins, delphiniums and dahlias, which gave her a huge palette of colour and season of interest to work with. Texture and shape, particularly of foliage, were also important to her and she popularized genera like *Funkia* (now called *Hosta*), *Bergenia* and others by using them in many imaginative and unusual combinations.

above Gertrude Jekyll's own garden at Munstead Wood. The vine (*Parthenocissus tricuspidata*) is beginning to colour, before a planting of asters and some silvery anaphalis.
left Around the lily pool at Folly Farm, Berkshire, grandly detailed architecture by Edwin Lutyens is softened by Jekyll's cascade of roses.

Woodland
and
Water

above Luxuriant plantings of big foliage like *Gunnera manicata* or *Rheum palmatum* lend excitement to even tiny pools, especially when combined with the narrow verticals of iris foliage (here *Iris kaempferi*), hostas, ferns and climbers. A stone wall gives a sense of enclosure, but an ivy-covered fence, a clipped hedge or a bank of shrubs would be just as effective.

right Drifts of autumn crocuses (species of *Colchicum*) lend enchantment to the autumn colours of the Japanese maple (one of many forms of *Acer palmatum*). Autumn crocuses add pinks, deep purples, mauves and white to the other colours of the season and naturalize easily.

SINCE PREHISTORIC TIMES, TREES AND WATER HAVE HAD symbolic power. The Tree of Life, whether a date palm, a quince tree, an apple or even a hawthorn, had a central place in many mythical gardens. It stood with the four rivers of the ancient world issuing from its roots, and ancient gardens would often feature a fountain or a tank of precious water at the centre, along with four water courses flowing from it.

In the Far East, bamboo, plum and pine have been known for at least 2,000 years as 'the three friends'. The bamboo stands for Buddha, the plum for Confucius, and the pine for Lao Tzu. Together with chrysanthemums and maples, they can be found painted on screens throughout China and Japan.

Woodland gardens, comprising both trees and the plants that grow beneath them, also have a long history in the West. The gardens of ancient Rome had deliberately planted woodlands decorated with rustic grottoes and altars to the gods of fertility. The tradition survived for many centuries, right through the Renaissance and the Age of Enlightenment, when many eighteenth-century gardens had, beyond the flowery parterres, plantings of wild cherry, hawthorn and lilac.

Wooded areas were created in American gardens, too with fine examples among the grand houses on the banks of the Hudson: Montgomery Place and Hyde Park were much admired by the American landscape designer Andrew Jackson Downing in the 1820s.

In the later nineteenth century, William Robinson advocated naturalistic plantings in his book *The Wild Garden* (1870), and Gertrude Jekyll used woodland flora to create plantings that are almost all classics now (see pages 52–3).

American designers are pre-eminent today in woodland design, particularly James van Sweden and Wolfgang Oehme, whose fine plantings exploit all levels of the woodland flora.

Water gardening is a modern phenomenon. In the past, when building pools or lakes was expensive, no gardener wanted the brilliant surface cluttered with water lilies and irises. But now it is fashionable to have water features brimming with life and the garden filled with wetland plants.

Ancient

Ancient oriental gardens often used water – or its symbolic representation – as a visual aid to contemplation. In the West, even the smallest Roman gardens usually incorporated water, whether in a tank to hold rainwater or in the form of a fountain fed from a communal water supply. Medieval Europe followed suit, with fountains designed by some of the greatest artists and architects.

As springs and pools were used primarily for drinking water, they were rarely planted, but a few classic combinations do derive from ancient times. Woodland flora, often richest around pools and springs, was admired and transplanted to the garden.

acer and azalea

In ancient Japan, there was already a huge range of variants of the maple *Acer palmatum* by the early seventeenth century, and its combination with azaleas and rhododendrons was well established.

The finely cut yellow-green foliage of the maple contrasts with a vibrant pink-flowered azalea, and is just as effective when the azalea flowers are gone: its sallow green oval leaves still set off the maple, and colour well in autumn. There are many grand cultivars of *Acer palmatum*; try *A. palmatum* 'Aureum' or the red-leaved *A. palmatum* 'Heptalobum Rubrum' with white azaleas, all set in a sea of trilliums.

cultivation Both plants like shade and shelter, and moist, though not sodden, soil enriched with peat and leafmould. The maple is a small tree, slow growing and easily pruned. The azalea makes a low mounded bush, easily kept in shape with light pruning after flowering.

extending the grouping In a small space, try a carpet of tiny grass like *Festuca glauca* or one of the small sedges like easy-to-grow 'Tauernpass'. In a larger garden, a bigger maple like *Acer ginnala* and some bamboos extend the Japanese theme.

water lilies and weeping willow

In ancient Persian gardens, the weeping willow symbolized Majnun, lover of the drowned Laila, the water lily. The vertical lines formed by the pendant branches of the weeping willow (*Salix babylonica*) and the horizontal emphasis of the water lilies (*Nymphaea* hybrids) make a perfect harmony. In cool climates, pure white or pale yellow water lilies (*Nymphaea* 'Marliacea Albida' or 'Marliacea Chromatella'), complement the pale green willow.

cultivation The pool needs to be at least 10m (33ft) across for the planting to be a success. Willows like wet ground, so the margins of a natural pool are best. The tree can be pollarded every two or three seasons to keep it under control. Some water lilies can be vigorous, too, though there are varieties that will grow in shallow water. Water lilies need sun to thrive, so the site must be open.

extending the grouping Drifts of Japanese irises will complete the scheme, and the addition of large foliage can be dramatic: *Gunnera manicata* if there's room; *Darmera peltata* if there isn't.

far left A tiny enclosed space suits the pairing of acer and azalea perfectly. It need not be Japanese in inspiration, but could feature gravel or mossy stones beneath, and a small pool.

left The ancient combination of water lilies and weeping willow receives a modern treatment in Monet's famous garden at Giverny, with wisteria-swathed bridges in the Japanese style and up-to-the-minute varieties of water lily.

In sixteenth-century Europe, water features were essential elements in many gardens, including (in the grandest), water parterres, fountains, rills, even ridged water chutes called 'chadars', based on Arabic models. Water was a status symbol and needed to be as clear and glittering as possible. This was largely true throughout the seventeenth century, too, but in the eighteenth century, as water in the landscape became less formal, gardeners began allowing water lilies to dot the surface, and irises and reeds to decorate the margins. Elsewhere in the garden, too, the development of the 'American garden' – traditionally a boggy, peaty, woodland area – meant that many new plant combinations began to appear.

snowdrops and crocuses

The appearance of snowdrops and crocuses has been gladdening the hearts of gardeners since the 1500s. Smart gardeners might think the combination dated, but with carefully chosen plants, it is breathtaking.

The golden rule is not to mix the two sorts of bulb too evenly. Plant each in drifts, in scale with the size of your garden. The combination suits small formal gardens quite as well as huge country ones. Both bulbs do well under trees or large shrubs; they will naturalize in grass and make ideal early plantings for large pots or tubs. I find some of the large-flowered Dutch crocuses too loud for the delicacy of the snowdrops; look out for *Crocus* species instead. *C. tommasinianus* is the earliest and comes in several delightful shades of purple. Try, too, *C. susianus* and *C. sieberi*. There are many varieties of snowdrop, though none as vigorous as the plain species, *Galanthus nivalis*.

cultivation Snowdrops are best planted in spring 'in the green', when the flowers are finished but the bulb is still in leaf, though dried bulbs will establish eventually. Crocuses, however, should be planted in autumn. Both genera produce many bulblets each season and

clumps can get so crowded that flowering stops. Ideally, you should divide clumps every three or four years.

extending the grouping Add daffodils (*Narcissus* 'February Silver'), especially amongst the coral-brown unfolding shoots of herbaceous paeonies. Complete the planting with semi-evergreen ferns like *Polystichum setiferum* and some early-flowering pulmonarias.

irises and azaleas

This is a marvel of woodland and water-edge planting and has been a feature of Japanese gardens for many centuries. This planting uses the splendid variegated form of wild flag iris (*Iris pseudacorus* 'Variegata'), combined with a woodland azalea (*Rhododendron*). The architectural shape of the iris, emphasized by golden lines of variegation, makes a perfect foil for the foliage and amber-and-buff flowers of the azalea. An added bonus is that the azalea foliage colours brilliantly in autumn.

Good azaleas, amongst the myriad old and new cultivars, include 'Magnificum', which is pale with rose-flushed buds and a lovely scent; 'Narcissiflorum', an intense yellow and also perfumed; and 'Palestrina', which is white, as is the enchanting species azalea, *Rhododendron occidentale*. The iris is irreplaceable, though in a drier part of the garden *Iris pallida* 'Variegata' could be attractively combined with yellow azaleas such as *R. luteum* or *R.* 'George Reynolds'.

cultivation Sun and dappled shade suit both species, which grow as well in an ordinary flower border as they will by a natural pool. Azaleas (all hybrids within the genus *Rhododendron*) like peaty and acid soils. The iris soon makes a large clump and can easily be propagated from its own seed, which should be sown in autumn and left to winter outdoors.

extending the grouping In a small space, add a haze of thalictrums, either *Thalictrum minus* or *T. aquilegiifolium*, and some bold foliage for contrast: perhaps pale-flowered bergenias like 'Brahms', or *Astilboides tabularis*. In a larger garden, try to find space for bamboos, ligularias and ferns.

astilbes and osmunda

rodgersias and primulas

This traditional pairing, in which the pink flowers and purplish foliage of the astilbes contrast with luxuriant summer ferns, is a highlight of the Sir Harold Hillier Gardens in Romsey, Hampshire. The combination has a long season; the osmunda has golden-brown autumn foliage and the flower spikes of the astilbe last, albeit brown coloured, until you clear them away. Hoar frost transforms them, adding another dimension. Astilbes range in colour from cream to deep red: try *Astilbe astilboides* 'Betsy Cuperus' or *A*. 'Amethyst'.

cultivation Both plants like moist, rich soil and light shade. They are also very hardy, although the most spectacular plants will be produced in warm gardens. Osmunda slowly makes large clumps which can be divided in spring. Alternatively, sow the spores on peat, then cover the pot with plastic film and keep in a shady place. Clumps of astilbes can be divided in spring or autumn.

extending the grouping The tall grass *Miscanthus sinensis,* with its bluish green leaves and pale flower plumes, makes a good background, while the linear leaves of *Iris sibirica* contrast with the ferns – use the pink-flowered 'Sparkling Rosé'.

A fine late nineteenth-century waterside combination of autumnal colours: carmine and bronze *Rodgersia podophylla* amongst the dead flower stems of *Primula sikkimensis*. The planting is just as effective in spring and summer, with the white froth of rodgersia flowers and the perfumed heads of yellow primulas. All the rodgersias are good foliage plants, varying mostly in the form of their leaves. *R*. 'Parasol', with pale green disc-shaped leaves, is more dependent on moisture than others. Other primulas worth trying include *P. florindae* and the scented *P. alpicola*.

cultivation Rodgersias need moist soil and will grow happily in light shade. The primula needs plenty of light to flourish so put it at the edge of the shade. Rodgersias increase slowly, but division is easy once you have a large plant. Seed germinates easily, too: keep seedlings in a nursery bed until big enough to plant out.

extending the grouping As here, add *Dryopteris filix-mas*, which keeps its foliage for most of the winter. Or plant purple *Iris ensata* hybrids at the water's edge, the ferns *Osmunda regalis* and *Matteucia struthiopteris*, and a sedge: try *Carex stricta* 'Bowles' Golden'.

far left
A combination of
Astilbe 'Erica',
Osmunda regalis ferns
and the shuttlecock
fern (*Matteucia
struthiopteris*).
left Rodgersias and
primulas suit a man-
made or natural pond.
below Primulas gone
to seed contrast with
the arching leaves of a
sedge. If your pool has
a waterproof lining,
add dryish-ground
plants like *Eryngium
planum* 'Tripartitum'
and *Geranium* x
riversleaianum
'Russell Prichard'.

primulas and sedges

The seedheads of primulas combine well with the arching leaves of
sedges, making a garden combination at its best in late summer. A
sunny, informal wildlife pond is the perfect site for these two
'marginals'. There are many bog-liking primulas: try *Primula alpicola*,
and hybrids like 'Inverewe'. The sedge *Carex pendula* has arching
flowerheads; try also sedges like the bur-reeds (*Sparganium erectum*).

cultivation Both plants like full sun and moist, even wet, peaty soil.
Both soon make big clumps, giving dense cover, and the sedge needs
to be thinned every few seasons. Primulas self-seed with abandon.
extending the grouping Add *Iris pseudacorus* var *bastardii* (its
flowers match the primula) and forms of *Iris kaempferi*.

hostas and
water lilies

Marginal and water plantings do not come much prettier than this: serried ranks of blue-green hosta leaves above the softly waved disc-like leaves and voluptuous flowers of the water lily – pictured is *Nymphaea* 'Marliacea Carnea'. Moisture-loving hostas are perfect partners to water lilies when planted by the side of pools – not only does the position suit the hostas' need for moist soil, but they also provide a transition between the pool and the rest of the garden.

This combination is equally at home in a formal pool in a sunny backyard as around a pond in the garden of a country house. It suits the tiniest of pools just as well as more spacious situations, but bear in mind when choosing a site that water lilies do not like fast-moving water or water splashed from fountains.

There are hundreds of hostas, from the huge *Hosta sieboldiana* var. *elegans* to wonders like *H. plantaginea* var. *japonica*, with splendid white, perfumed flowers. There are also many water lilies to choose from. Partner a blue hosta with pinks like *Nymphaea* 'Marliacea Carnea' or *N.* 'Masaniello'; with a green hosta, plant yellow *N.* 'Odorata Sulphurea', or even deepest pink *N.* 'Laydekeri Lilacea'.

cultivation The planting needs an open position, as water lilies require plenty of sun. Match the hosta to the situation and don't try golden or variegated leaf types, which can burn in full sunshine. To grow this lushly, hostas need fairly rich and moist soil, and constant war on the slug population if the leaves are not to be damaged. A similarly sized bank of hostas needs at least eight or nine plants to get established, but clumps are easily divided each season to make more. The planting depth of the water lily, and the size of its container, depend on the variety you use.

extending the grouping Water lily foliage contrasts well with the narrow oval floating leaves of aponogeton, which has perfumed flowers, too, and the lanceolate uprights of pontederia. I'd add the astonishingly tall variegated rush *Schoenoplectus lacustris* 'Albescens' or *S. lacustris* ssp. *tabernaemontani* 'Zebrinus' (in which the variegation shows as golden rings) for some vertical interest.

bluebells and honesty

Bluebells (*Hyacinthoides non-scripta*) and honesty (*Lunaria annua*) are a medieval pairing: tough, shade tolerant, even rather invasive, with the combination of purple and blue making a sumptuous start to the delights of summer. An underplanting of bluebells and honesty suits light woodland or the ground beneath large shrubs, though the combination is every bit as successful in a cottage garden or city yard.

For perfume, try the perennial *Lunaria rediviva*, with palest violet flowers followed by oval seed pods. To add variety to the bluebells, *Hyacinthoides hispanica* has flowers in washy pink or white, and a slightly coarser shape.

cultivation Bluebells can be grown from seed in a nursery bed, or obtained from friends. Grow the annual honesty from seed. Both plants tolerate shade and poor soil, though not drought.

extending the grouping *Anemone blanda* 'White Splendour' adds brilliance, as shown, so does a pale yellow erythronium.

previous page An elegant combination of hostas and water lilies.

above A pairing of bluebells and honesty is the perfect complement to other woodland plants.

right A tapestry hedge combining two forms of beech gives stylish shelter.

far right Combining philadelphus and weigela was possible once the latter had arrived from Japan in the late 1800s.

philadelphus and weigela

Popular since at least 1880, this traditional pairing is a common feature of both European and American gardens. The pink flowers and often rather spreading form of the weigela are a brilliant foil for the tall arching philadelphus branches and their white and often heavily perfumed flowers.

The combination makes a fine planting, even an informal hedge, for the front garden, especially for houses of the 1920s and 1930s. Keep to the green-leaved forms of each species: philadelphus flowers are hardly visible against yellow or variegated foliage, while weigela blossom clashes nastily with its purple-leaved or variegated species.

Ideally, use a large philadelphus variety, like 'Beauclerk' or 'Polar Star', and plant weigelas in front. The best reds include W. 'Bristol Ruby' and W. 'Newport Red'; the ordinary form of the species *Weigela florida*, from Japan, is excellent too.

cultivation Both shrubs are easy to grow, like good soil, and often tolerate quite heavy shade: indeed, the variegated forms of both burn badly in full sun. For best results, both species should be pruned after they have flowered. If you decide to plant a whole hedge, you will find weigela and philadelphus easy to propagate by cuttings.

extending the grouping Plant beneath white-flowered cherries or almonds, and over a ground planting of epimediums and scilla (see page 62). Add some tall bearded irises in bronzes and plums.

tapestry hedge of beech

Ancient hedgerows contained many species of hedging plants and nineteenth-century gardeners such as William Robinson copied the idea to make tapestry hedges. One of the classics is a mix of green-leaved and purple- (or 'copper'-) leaved beech (*Fagus sylvatica*). The combination works perfectly from spring to early autumn, when the contrasting foliage is at its brightest.

Beech tapestry hedges make ideal divisions in the garden, perhaps separating flower garden from woodland, or enclosing a rectangular lawn with a formal pool. Beech has greedy roots, so don't use it to back flower borders.

There are white- and yellow-variegated forms of beech and these can also be used to make ornamental hedges. Green and yellow-green yew, such as *Taxus baccata* 'Aureum', are possibilities, though the contrast can be too strong for many smaller gardens.

cultivation Beech needs to be planted in good soil to promote early growth, and performs best in sun or light shade. Space the plants around 1m (3ft) apart and, if you plan to grow a tall hedge, plant a double row. To achieve the tapestry effect, every fifth or sixth plant should be copper-leaved. A hedge like this will need cutting two or three times in a season. There is no upper limit to size, but do not use it for anything much less than 2m (6½ft) high and 1m (3ft) thick or the effect you are aiming for will be lost.

extending the grouping Holly can add glitter – as well as spines to deter intruders. Yew is also a natural addition, with its dark evergreen foliage (try adding *Tropaeolum speciosum*, too, see page 28). Both holly and yew will extend the season of the combination, making it look spectacular well into the winter.

Designer

With the advent of new water lily varieties from China and Japan, and hybrids being raised by many French nurseries, plus the availability of Japanese irises, many late nineteenth-century gardeners began to make plantings combining the two species. Monet's paintings did much to popularize both.

In recent times, the impetus of the late nineteenth century has continued, and while every garden centre stocks some of the plants I've selected, some designers are still exploring fresh aspects of the flora, from unusual grasses and sedges to new primulas and lythrums. American designers have a liking for woodland, allowing tree plantings and flora to grow up to the windows of houses or offices.

More attention is now being paid to ecological planting, and many gardeners like the idea of recreating in their own private spaces the nature that is slowly being eroded beyond the garden gate.

ferns and hostas

Ferns and hostas are made for one another, many ferns liking exactly the kinds of conditions in which hostas thrive, and their often complex leaf shape making a perfect foil for the bold and simple foliage of the hostas. Gertrude Jekyll was one of the first designers to make use of hostas (called funkias in her day), for although one or two were known in the eighteenth century, most reached Europe in the late 1800s. Despite the large numbers of fancy ferns that became available following the Victorian craze for them in the 1860s, she tended to use fairly common species.

The versatility of this combination means that it looks just as good in a formal urban space as in the most informal of gardens, and there are ferns and hostas for almost every situation: from small species for shaded and sheltered windowboxes or big pots, to large ones that will make an impact by a big pond or pool – a well-fed *Hosta sieboldiana elegans* can have leaves a metre (one yard) long.

There are very large numbers of fern genera and species available to experiment with, and many species vary enormously. Common ones, such as the male fern (*Dryopteris filix-mas*), the common polypody (*Polypodium vulgare*) and shield ferns (*Polystichum*), have leaves variously frilled, crested and so on. Many of these variants are interesting, and some can be very beautiful, although in some cases the simple perfection of nature's own design can appear to have become somewhat over-complicated.

Amongst the myriad hostas, remember that variegated and yellow-leaved forms need shade and, quite often, shelter. Some hostas are no more than 15cm (6in) tall; some have curled and twisted leaves; others can be marvellously ribbed. Cultivars like 'Royal Standard' are worth growing for their flowers, too.

cultivation Most ferns and all hostas will grow in shade and many will tolerate deep shade. Some will also tolerate dryish conditions, though most prefer moist, even wet, soil. In general, hostas tend to be hardy; but it is advisable to check that the ferns you use are suited to your area. Garden ferns are notably pest-and disease-proof. Unfortunately, hostas are the preferred food of snails and slugs: ensuring that your garden has plenty of frogs and toads will help to keep leaves unblemished.

Some ferns increase by runners, other have bulbils or tiny plantlets on the fronds, while some can only be increased by sowing the spores. Fill a translucent plastic tub with a couple of centimetres or so of moist compost, and place on top a fragment of frond with brown sporangia showing on the undersurface or on the frond margins. Put a lid on the tub, and place outdoors in a cool and shaded position. Fronds of new plantlets can take a year to show. Hostas can be easily increased by dividing clumps in spring, or, if you want new sorts, by collecting and sowing seed.

extending the grouping Good additions include any of the rodgersias, almost any astilbes (pale lilac ones complement blue-leaved hostas perfectly), irises, alliums, aquilegias – a generous drift of the yellow *Aquilegia aurea* or *A. chrysantha* 'Yellow Queen' looks fine amongst *Hosta plantaginea* or *H. tokudama* forms – and evergreen irises, especially *Iris foetidissima*.

above There are many variegated hostas, but you can't go far wrong with 'standards' like *H.* 'Thomas Hogg', or *H. fortunei* var. *aureomarginata*, or with easy ferns like *Dryopteris filix-mas*.
centre Varieties of *Polystichum setiferum*, a tough and semi-evergreen fern, vary in the density of their brown. It works well with a carpet of tiny *Hosta lancifolia*.
below Hosta flowers are available in shades of purple or in white; some varieties can be quite spectacular, and some have an attractive perfume.
overleaf *Hosta undulata* var. *univittata* together with other hybrids, makes an attractive underplanting for trees or shrubs, and works well with any of the pinnate-leaved ferns, thalictrums, aquilegias or dicentras.

day lilies and
alchemilla

Lady's mantle (*Alchemilla mollis*) did not arrive in western Europe until the late nineteenth century, when it was taken up enthusiastically by many garden designers including Gertrude Jekyll. She used it with the old-fashioned day lily, *Hemerocallis* 'Europa', in a combination that contrasts the soft green, lobed foliage of the alchemilla and its frothy yellow-green flowers with the linear arcs of the day lily leaves and its buff-orange flowers. The combination is also used on either side of brick paths at Hidcote in Gloucestershire, in the gardens designed by Lawrence Johnston.

A shaded, urban front garden would benefit equally from this planting or it could be set around a garden pond. I have also seen the two plants used in combination with pale pink day lilies beneath a grove of high-pruned lilac bushes.

Other species of alchemilla are available, but all are smaller and less tolerant of shade. Day lilies are legion: in the main, choose only tall-growing sorts, though the floppy *Hemerocallis lilioasphodelus* looks excellent with alchemilla and has a delicious perfume.

cultivation Both plants do well in damp shade and are equally vigorous in full sun. Alchemilla flowers from summer onwards; if the plants get too congested, simply chop back to the creeping stem and in a few weeks fresh green foliage will appear. This also stops the flowers setting seed, thus avoiding a surfeit of seedlings. Day lilies are best propagated by division in either autumn or spring. Keep slugs and snails in check in early spring to prevent damage to young leaves.

extending the grouping Clumps of the cream-flowered *Aruncus dioicus* and a solidago can be included for autumn colour, as shown. But for a Jekyll 'look' add ferns and the big glossy leaves of bergenias – their vivid flowers will be over long before the day lily blooms and their colour will be much softened by the alchemilla.

far left Day lilies are good shade plants; if you can't find 'Europa', pictured here, try a yellow variety such as 'Whichford', which also has elegant flower shapes.

left This combination of day lilies and alchemilla is set off by peltiphyllums and water lilies, making an attractive view from a window or terrace.

below A luxuriant planting of hellebores and Solomon's seal, whose leaves make airy supports for the strings of flowers.

hellebores, and
solomon's seal

Margery Fish's garden at East Lambrook Manor in Somerset still contains many of her splendid planting ideas: this one is beneath pollarded willows in what she called her 'ditch garden'. It consists of stands of Solomon's seal (*Polygonatum* x *hybridum)*, and masses of hellebores (*Helleborus orientalis*). It is perfect along a narrow shady path, either through woodland or leading to your front door.

cultivation Both plants are hardy and prefer damp soil with summer shade, but they will cope in a border with some shade or – as in my garden – with no sun at all, but rich soil. The pairing is nearly pest- and disease-proof; slugs do occasionally damage the Solomon's seal.
extending the grouping In my garden, I have added white *Lilium candidum* and set the whole planting beneath an old apple tree.

cotinus and clematis

The purple-leaved form of the smokebush (*Cotinus coggygria* 'Royal Purple'), a fine shrub growing to 3m (10ft) high, is here combined with the pendant young flowers of *Clematis* 'Etoile Rose', a planting which was first used in the 1930s. This is a combination for a shady shrubbery or, even better, an urban front yard, where a high-value planting is needed.

cultivation Cotinus is easy to grow, happy in sun or shade, glorious when in leaf and when in flower, and still going strong in autumn, as the leaves turn scarlet and burgundy along the veins. The clematis dies back to the ground each season; clear stems away in early to mid-spring when you can see new growth. It is rather rare: if you have

difficulty tracking it down, the similar 'Gravetye Beauty,' which was introduced by William Robinson in 1914, is easier to find. It, too, sometimes dies back to the base; check when you clear the dead stems away, as it can build up old wood which needs to be taken out.

extending the grouping Surround with a lush planting of geraniums, such as *Geranium sylvaticum* 'Mayflower', as seen below, or *G. pratense*: 'Mrs Kendall Clark' is often blue or pale violet. I would add *G. phaeum*, which is blackish purple in the species and pale in cultivars like 'Lily Lovell'.

The green-leaved variety of the cotinus is easy from seed and, if anything, lovelier than the purple cultivar: in summer it has a pinkish-green 'smoke' of flower sprays; in autumn the leaves turn an intense scarlet. It looks good paired with the late-flowering *Clematis* 'Huldine' in silvery-pink, amidst clumps of the equally late-flowering and non-climbing *C.* x *bonstedtii* 'Côte d'Azur', which is silver-blue.

meconopsis and primulas

Grand plantings of meconopsis and candelabra primulas can be seen in shady woodland gardens all over the temperate world. There is a subtle affinity between the translucent, pleated blue petals of the poppy *Meconopsis betonicifolia* and the tiers of richly coloured, substantial primula flowers, often in shades of rusty pink or hot reds. The mix can give tremendous excitement to a garden.

Try the combination by a woodland seat or as a drift planting along a rivulet or ditch. Some of the primulas, especially *Primula pulverulenta* and its many hybrids, plus 'lovelies' like *P. florindae* and *P. helodoxa*, will grow right to the water's edge if you have a natural pool.

Meconopsis betonicifolia is an attractive and reliable plant, though there are grander ones available to try as well. For the primulas, as a start, try brick-red 'Inverewe'.

cultivation In cool gardens, all meconopsis will enjoy dappled sun and moist soil; elsewhere, both poppies and primulas need assured moisture and shade. With some care, both are easy to grow from seed, providing enough plants to set out in some quantity. Both are winter hardy, and largely pest-and disease-proof, though vine weevil can decimate both if allowed to rampage unchecked.

extending the grouping Any of the damp-ground ferns add charm to the planting, especially the shuttlecock fern (*Matteucia struthiopteris*), with its brilliant green young foliage, or the tough and creeping 'sensitive fern' (*Onoclea sensibilis*), with its broad olive-green foliage that will darken to rusty brown in autumn. Add almost any of the non-variegated hostas, flag irises (*Iris pseudacorus* can show various shades of yellow flowers as well as variegated foliage) and Siberian irises such as 'White Swirl', 'Pink Haze' and the violet 'Lady Vanessa'. The whole assemblage makes an attractive underplanting for lovely flowering dogwoods such as *Cornus florida* 'White Cloud' and *C. florida* 'Apple Blossom'.

epimediums and scillas

The delightful ground-cover combination of the pale but intense yellow flowers of *Epimedium pinnatum* and the dusky blue of *Scilla bifolia* was used by Graham Stuart Thomas to underplant the fascinating and little-known shrub *Stachyurus praecox*. *Scilla bifolia* is much underused. If you can't find it, try the paler and earlier-flowering *S. mischtschenkoana*, which works with other species of epimedium, some of which have amber or even rusty-pink flowers. The foliage of all these plants is a sheer delight.

cultivation Leave the epimedium foliage untouched in winter to contrast with the linear leaves of the scilla; you will still see enough of the flowers. Epimediums increase quite well, like shade, and tolerate dry soil. Scillas increase freely from seed.

extending the grouping If you grow hazels, plant a sheet of scillas and epimediums in your nuttery.

dicentra and euphorbia

A pretty planting by the English gardener Margery Fish, who loved the old-fashioned bleeding heart (*Dicentra spectabilis*) far more than the recent introductions. Writing in the 1960s, she said she was sorry to see it was falling out of fashion. She also liked the brilliant green-yellow of *Euphorbia polychroma*. Here the two are combined, the arching sprays of acid-pink and white bleeding heart contrasting strongly with the equally acidic yellow of the euphorbia. The combination is kept together by the soft green of the dicentra leaves.

cultivation Both plants like cool moist conditions; the dicentra needs shelter, too, as the flowering stems are fragile. Otherwise, both are easy to grow, flower in late spring and thrive on rich feeding.

extending the grouping Add one of the fern and hosta combinations on pages 52–4, or an iris like 'Holden Clough'.

ligularias and macleayas

For drama around the pondside, or in any sheltered area with damp soil, this early twentieth-century combination can hardly be bettered. The tall plume poppy (*Macleaya cordata* and forms of *M. microcarpa*), with its large smoky-grey foliage and cream or pinkish flowers, is teamed with *Ligularia stenocephala* (though the similar *L.* 'The Rocket' is somewhat easier to find), whose dark green foliage, often purple beneath, makes a handsome base to the tall spires of yellow flowers.

Though both plants are large – the plume poppy can reach up to 2.5m (8ft) – they are worth considering for adding scale and style to a border by a path, a damp patch in a shrubbery or light woodland.

cultivation These plants are good growers, neither needing staking, though shelter from wind is helpful. The plume poppy can be invasive; ligularias are less so, but still increase quickly. Both plants like rich soil that is moist but not waterlogged.

extending the grouping Phloxes in rose-pink or shrill mauves look stunning in autumn, once the yellow ligularia flowers have faded and as the plume poppy foliage begins to colour more subtly.

Claude Monet

right Water lilies have always had special significance. The enchanting ones here are all hybrids. In central Europe *Nymphaea alba* was once believed to keep away evil spirits, while Buddhists from India to China have venerated the blue *Nymphaea stellata*.

far right below
The flat lily pads, often beautifully marked in bronze and green, and the green-painted punt emphasize the horizontal plane of the water, and break up its brilliant surface. The arched bridge and the luxuriant lakeside planting add to the picturesque scene.

MONET LIVED AT GIVERNY FROM 1883 TO 1926, IN THE EARLY YEARS AS AN improverished tenant, and by the later ones as a wealthy and successful owner. Both garden and house are now faithful recreations, following some neglect during the 1930s and 1940s.

The area called the Clos Normand was Monet's earliest garden here, and he divided it into rectangular planting areas to each side of the famous central walk. Though first designed as a kitchen garden to feed the family, it eventually became filled with flowers for cutting, starting with tulips, jonquils and narcissus, and ending with a blaze of dahlias and roses.

He bought the land for the water garden in 1895 and, as soon as the pools were excavated and filled from the nearby stream, he began planting water lilies and weeping willows. Monet used the latest hybrid water lilies at Giverny. Hybridization had only begun a decade or so before, when subtropical American and Chinese species arrived in Europe, and their flower colours were at once bred into the white-flowered, but hardy, European species like *Nymphaea alba* and *N. candida*.

Visitors, especially influential critics, patrons and politicians, soon began to arrive, and the garden started to appear in major magazines, like the British *Country Life*, in the 1920s.

Monet's design of the richly planted water garden was an influential moment in gardening, marking the change from water being used as a predominantly architectural feature to a place to grow plants. He filled the pool margins with Japanese irises, pontederias, ferns and hostas, creating a luxuriance we all now seek.

above Wisteria stems twine around their metal support on the bridge at Giverny. The bridge frames the views of the lake and its lilies, and of the surrounding planting.

Kitchen Gardens

above This wild but fruitful tangle of different shades of green from chards, cabbages, kales and vines is an ideal way of growing produce for the kitchen, and is visually satisfying. The vines are grown on a low framework, making pruning and protection from birds easy, while at the same time creating shelter for young vegetables.

right Silver, gold and blue-green from young artichokes, tagetes and savoy cabbages make handsome and tidy rows in the garden. Tagetes are reputed to keep aphids and other harmful insects away, though experiments by Joy Larkcom suggest the effect, if any, is very slight.

KITCHEN AND HERB GARDENS HAVE BEEN CORE elements of gardening since the beginning of civilization: the cultivation of food was an important factor in enabling mankind to settle in one place. Kitchen gardens are still central to much of gardening: the increasing modern fascination with potagers is an attempt to re-integrate kitchen garden plants with the sort of decorative gardening that has been in the ascendant for the past century and a half.

Kitchen gardens have strong links with the past. Well-organized ones are commonly divided into four sections to allow crop rotation, and the old four-square layout goes back well beyond the walled kitchen gardens of the eighteenth and nineteenth centuries. This traditional form of garden layout can be traced back through the hedged or ditched and moated kitchen gardens of the sixteenth and seventeenth centuries, through medieval cloister gardens and Roman ones, right back to the very earliest gardens of Mesopotamia.

Modern gardeners, like their forebears, are again beginning to collect varieties of fruit and vegetables, both to preserve them for the future and to enjoy the flavours that current, mass-produced varieties may lack. The increasing range also allows some very decorative effects, whether in the re-creation of ancient potagers or something much more modern.

New gardeners are discovering that a well-tended kitchen garden, whether traditional or avant-garde, gives as much pleasure as any rose bed and provides treats for the table, too.

Ingenuity is all: you can have fun with kitchen plant combinations even if you are restricted to a roof garden or just a balcony with room for a vine in a pot, and some containers of bronze-leaved chicories, nasturtiums and a borage plant.

Modern gardeners imitate sixteenth-century arbours of vine or trained apple trees, or use tunnels to display squashes and beans. Some copy nineteenth-century methods of pruning fruit trees to make exotic shapes. All give vertical emphasis.

In a garden with a ground-work of salads and vegetables, edge the beds or paths with parsley or alpine strawberries, and give the garden emphatic horizontal elements too.

Ancient

Ancient Eygyptian frescos show gardens fringed with date palms, with ibis stalking the water channels, and rows of fine vegetables: cos lettuces, brassicas and radishes. Excavations in Roman cities like Pompeii suggest salads were grown in rows, shaded by vines and lemons. Throughout the Orient, bamboo shoots, lotus roots and chrysanthemum petals became part of the repertoire. In the Americas, only a few edible species, like the potato, became used in artistic imagery, and give any insight into probable plantings.

squash, beans and corn

This combination probably dates back to pre-Columbian Central America – along the way it has acquired the folk name of 'The Three Sisters'. It is a mutually beneficial planting – the swift-growing squash or pumpkin plants give shelter to the corn and beans in spring, and later in the season the beans provide nitrogen to support the luxuriant growth of corn and squash. In autumn, the backdrop of corn haulms emphasizes the golden rotundity of the ripe squashes. There are some extraordinary varieties of corn, with scarlet or mahogany seeds or even multi-coloured cobs, and many pumpkins and squashes, from striped and ridged 'Turks Cap' types to a palette of colours that includes cinnamon-brown skin, green warts and brilliant orange flesh.

cultivation Sow all three plants under glass in early spring. Sow extra corn and beans, as the rampant squash plants need to be heavily outnumbered to stop them taking over. Choose a site in rich soil in full sun, and water everything copiously. Few varieties of corn will produce much of a crop in cool gardens, though a sunny site will give fine crops of squashes, pumpkins and beans.

extending the grouping To carry on a South and Central American theme add ordinary nasturtiums or perhaps the dark red variety 'Empress of India'.

above This planting makes a good screen for a compost pit, or a shelter for a rough seat. Its rather ramshackle appearance suits an informal garden better than a neatly formal one.

far right Though many other cabbages are also handsome, the 'Cavalo Nero' is unique. There are different strains of marigolds on the market – this one is called 'Art Shades'.

black cabbage and
marigolds

These two ancient garden plants make a striking combination: the marigold (Calendula), cultivated for so long that it has lost any connection with a wild species, and the handsome 'Cavolo Nero', the black cabbage, a primitive loose-leaved, non-heading type, standing palm-tree fashion well above them. Its dark green 'Savoy-like' foliage contrasts in colour and texture with the golden marigold flowers.

The combination is certainly medieval, probably much earlier. It works well in the kitchen garden or potager and can be continued right through to the table: the black cabbage is delicious when lightly steamed and tastes even better with a scattering of marigold petals.

As a bedding scheme, it will last well into winter and could be planted as an unusual edging in a cottage garden or perhaps backed with *Rosa gallica* var. *officinalis*.

cultivation Sow the black cabbage in early to mid-spring in nursery beds outside, or in a pot under glass. The seedlings can then be set out at final spacings in late spring. Marigolds need no special treatment and are easily sown directly in the open ground. Both crops need sun and rich, well-drained soil. The cabbage will be ready to harvest in summer.

extending the grouping The dark-toned leaves of the cabbage offset the jagged silver foliage of cardoons or globe artichokes to good effect and the bed could be edged with clipped rosemary hedges or bands of white- or purple-flowered chives.

Traditional

Vegetable growing was so much a part of many peoples' lives well into the present century that there are many traditional combinations still around. Some are derived from real or imagined cultural needs of the plants, others from ideas about 'companion planting' and the natural compatibility of the two plants, and yet others began simply because most gardeners thought they looked good that way.

bronze fennel and day lilies

Bronze fennel (*Foeniculum vulgare* 'Purpureum', a form of the wild European species) and the ancient Japanese form of day lily (*Hemerocallis fulva*) make a gorgeous combination, the dark filigree fennel leaves showing off the simple form of the brightly-coloured flowers to perfection. The day lily flowers for a long season – though as its name implies, each flower lasts for just one day – and will overlap with the flat sprays of greenish yellow fennel flowers. This particular day lily reached Europe in the sixteenth century from China, where it is known as 'The Flower of Forgetfulness' – the blooms are cooked and eaten to assuage an unhappy memory. The combination could be of the same date.

cultivation Both the fennel and day lily are tough perennials that like fertile, well-drained soil, though they are also able to tolerate poor conditions. Divide clumps of day lilies after a few years; the fennel will produce as many seedlings as you need as well as giving you plenty to give away.

extending the grouping Bronze fennel looks stunning with deep pink roses, or shrub species like the deliciously scented eglantine – this combination comes into its own again in autumn with the rust-red hips of the rose against the dark foliage. Add *Euphorbia palustris* and perhaps the pink-flowered variant of cow parsley (*Anthriscus sylvestris*) or another umbellifer like *Myrrhis odorata*.

lavender and thyme

This heavenly scented combination contrasts low-growing sheets of purple-flowered thyme (*Thymus*) with the silvery-grey upright bushes of lavender (*Lavandula*), a combination used in herb gardens for many years. It looks as good over an acre as it does in a square yard around a sunny garden seat. There are huge numbers of thyme species and hybrids; some make small shrubs, some ground-hugging carpets; others have different smells and coloured or variegated leaves. Lavenders are less variable, but try some of the pink shades and, in mild gardens, more tender species: *Lavandula dentata* is a delight.

cultivation Both plants need sun, poorish soil, and will thrive in dry gardens. A sheltered area is best. Some thymes will grow in paving but most do best planted out in soil. Lavenders eventually get leggy and woody, so take cuttings every season so that you always have young plants ready to replace old ones.

extending the grouping Add non-invasive aromatics like pennyroyal (*Mentha pulegium*) or *Calamintha grandiflora*. Old-fashioned pinks such as the annual *Dianthus* 'Loveliness' work well.

alliums and artichokes

The huge jagged and silver-green leaves of globe artichokes (*Cynara scolymus*) or closely related cardoons (*C. cardunculus*) associate well with species of allium, whether it be in a traditional planting of ordinary chives (*Allium schoenoprasum*) or when combined with leeks (*A. porrum*) left to flower. Leeks have soft mauve balls of flowers that complement the silvery foliage of the artichoke and look even more dramatic when the first artichoke heads begin to show.

Try this planting in a bed perhaps 3.7m (12ft) square, the centre filled with five or six artichoke plants, surrounded by a generous band of chives (infinitely more than you could ever use in the kitchen), and a margin of love-in-a-mist, or even beetroot or ruby chard. Add a bean-entwined bower over a rustic seat for a delightful and productive garden. Chinese chives or white-flowered ones make good alternatives, but no other kitchen garden plant has foliage to rival that of artichokes or cardoons.

cultivation Grow the artichokes from seed sown singly in pots in early spring. Alternatively, take side shoots sliced from the periphery of mature plants. Plant out the artichokes at 1.2m (4ft) spacing; they are not fully hardy, and many need winter protection with cloches or a blanket of leaves. Chives are easily grown from seed and make clumps that split readily to give huge numbers of new plants. Leeks should be started off indoors, then later planted out at 30–45cm (1–1½ft) intervals. They will overwinter except in very cold gardens and may go on to produce new side bulbs at ground level, which make delicious eating.

extending the grouping After the first cropping from the artichokes, the plants look messy until the next wave of foliage forms. Underplanting them with buckler-leaf sorrel (*Rumex scutatus*) is a clever way to make a leafy and tough background that yields another crop when you clear away the untidy artichoke foliage. Woodland strawberries are a pretty and useful addition, too. In a bigger bed, a central stand of amber-coloured sunflowers (*Helianthus annuus*) would be fun, or even a large rhubarb plant.

previous page If you are unable to find the day lily shown here (*Hemerocallis* 'Europa'), a dusty-pink form such as 'Pink Damask' will look equally good.

far left
This combination can be formal, with the lavenders shaped into hedges, or more relaxed, with large lavenders such as 'Giant White'.

above left
Artichokes and flowering leeks complement each other. Roman gardens could not keep pace with the demand for artichokes and gourmets had to import them from North Africa. Apparently the emperor Nero ate leeks several times a month in order to 'clear his voice'.

below left
Artichokes and chives grown in the eighteenth-century manner. Chives may have been gathered from wild populations before becoming a garden plant in the sixteenth century.

cabbages and alliums

The combination of cabbages and other brassicas with the various relatives of the humble leek and onion from the genus *Allium* have long been a traditional feature of the kitchen garden. It comes into its own from high summer, when decorative kales, chives (*Allium schoenoprasum*) and masses of the varigated nasturtium 'Alaska' can make an enchanting picture, right through to late autumn, when a splendid traditional winter combination contrasts the linear leaves of leeks (*Allium porrum*) with the broad and veined leaves of the brassicas, whether kitchen kales or winter cabbages.

The combination works as well in a formal potager as it does in a much more informal arrangement and, depending on the varieties used, fits into a smaller garden just as well as a more expansive plot. Both crops will last through all but the worst frosts and will look good well into early winter.

There are many sorts of decorative kale – 'Coral Queen' is a good one – but others make better eating, like the dramatic 'Russian Red', or even the hardy blue-leaved curly kale, in which case you could try adding some blue violas – the flowers are edible. Cabbages like

above Edible, strong-flavoured decorative kale is mixed with chives and combined with a variegated nasturtium (look out for 'Alaska').

right The blue-green leaves of the leeks provide a contrast with the leaves of summer cabbages.

far right Three sorts of cabbage grown in parallel strips showing different colours, leaf textures and veining.

'January King' (which is blue-green and flushed with purple) would also complement the colour scheme.

If you want to copy the planting on pages 66–7 with its sumptuous colours, use the red-leaved Brussels sprout called 'Rubine' and one of the 'January King' group of cabbages, though some of the old red cabbages would also look stunning. The leek is one of the legion of blue-green leaved sorts – 'Musselburgh' is a good example.

The colour scheme could easily be reversed, using a red-leaved leek, and deep green Savoy cabbages or sprouts. European cabbages present a vast range of variants, with spring and summer varieties and winter-hardy sorts with solid hearts. Foliage can vary from pale green and lustrous deep greens, to deep greens shaded with purple, and on to deep reds. Leaf texture can be smooth and waxy, or crinkled between the veins like the 'Savoy' group, with a number of intermediates. Oriental cabbages offer even more variation.

cultivation All the plants like sun and good soil. Start leeks and brassicas off early in the season in a greenhouse or in a seed bed under a cloche. Once the seedlings have been planted out, but before they get too big, use the surrounding ground for quick-maturing combinations like radishes and spinach, or a mix of coloured-leaf lettuces and mizuna greens such as the combination of mizuna and mustard on page 83.

Alternatively, brassicas can be started off by sowing a couple of seeds at each spot in the kitchen garden where you are in need of a mature plant. Once the seedlings have a few leaves, thin them out, leaving one only at each 'station' – the culled seedlings are delicious. If you want nasturtiums, too, sow seed in late spring in the open ground; the plants are vigorous, and you will find you need to set a seed only every few feet.

Chives, spring onions and shallots do not grow well in shade, so make sure they are not shaded by nearby plants or buildings.

extending the grouping For height, add a group of sweetcorn plants or a tripod of climbing beans. For changes in scale of foliage, use the combination around squash or pumpkin plants, especially ones with orange or green-striped fruit. If you find that the chives get swamped, then next season try planting leeks or Welsh onions.

Designer

Renaissance painters explored the use of fruits and vegetables to make strange portrait pictures, but contemporary garden designers like Joy Larkcom in England and Frederica Philip in Canada have led the field in exploring the possibilities of fruits and vegetables, adding flowers and making exciting new combinations. Even kitchen gardeners used to turnips and carrots are considering the opportunities offered by oca, mibuna and mizuna greens, orach and amaranthus, and discovering that it is easy to have as much colour in a kitchen garden as in a flower garden

fennel and sunflowers

A delightful modern combination of two tall kitchen garden crops – sunflower *(Helianthus annuus)* can be grown for its edible seeds and contrasts its coarse heart-shaped foliage and warm amber flowers with the green filigree of the fennel leaf *(Foeniculum vulgare)*. The eventual appearance of the greeny-yellow umbels of fennel flowers improves the combination further. This planting makes a charming flower garden combination and works as well for a cottage garden as a sunny town one.

cultivation Both plants need sun and rich, fairly moist soil. Fennel is easy to grow from seed; it may take a season or two to mature, but once established it is a strong perennial and plants should be set at least 1m (3ft) apart. The sunflowers are annuals and in warm areas can be sown directly into the ground; in cool gardens start them off singly in small pots in early spring. Unlike the single-stemmed varieties that produce just one flower, 'Velvet Queen' branches and gives a good show of flowers from each plant.

extending the grouping In a kitchen garden, site the combination alongside the jagged foliage of squashes, small pumpkins or cardoons; in a flower garden, try it in a sea of lemon-yellow nasturtiums.

left Fennel and sunflowers are both very vigorous and you will need to keep them away from less dynamic neighbours. In this picture, green fennel is combined with the warm amber flowers of the sunflower 'Velvet Queen', but the effect of the combination could be altered by combining purplish-leaved bronze fennel with strains of sunflower like 'Prado Red' or 'Holiday', or the seed strain 'Autumn Beauty'.

overleaf
A sumptuous and highly productive planting, in which artichokes, asparagus, runner beans and sweetcorn are combined with deep bronze sunflowers, some lovely scarlet day lilies, euphorbias and anthemis.

right Grown here on a conifer, this pair of climbers – *Clematis* 'The President' and the purple-podded pea – is equally good clambering through an old pink climbing rose or bush rose, say 'Ville de Bruxelles' or 'The Garland', or a white like 'Iceberg' or 'Mme. Plantier'.

far right A winter salad can be made with the frilled leaves of mizuna, which are able to stand a few degrees of frost. The red mustard is equally hardy, but can taste very peppery.

purple peas and clematis

This witty planting of two unlikely companions – a purple-flowered clematis ('The President') and the old purple-podded pea, a variety of *Pisum sativum* – makes a captivating tangle on a conifer. A sunny fence, a rose arch or a doorway presents the perfect site. The pea can reach a height of 3m (10ft).

cultivation Some peas are winter hardy and so can be planted in autumn, but the purple-podded pea is best planted in spring, indoors or under glass, with seeds sown singly in pots. Once they are cropping, keep harvesting the peas, or they will begin to ripen and suppress a further crop and the combination will not last very long.

Clematis 'The President' must be cut down to within 90cm (3ft) of the soil surface in late winter in order to produce the maximum number of flowers. Both plants like rich soil and plenty of water.

extending the grouping To add tones of red, try the amber-red of the easy-to-grow climber *Eccremocarpus scaber*, or dusky-red *Phygelius aequalis*; if you want something really startling, try planting the combination over the wall shrub *Crinodendron hookerianum*.

The purple-podded pea is the only pea with unusual pods, but among the climbing French beans or pole beans there are some very dramatically podded varieties, including many purples, some fine yellows and ivories, and some splashed in green and red. 'Blue Peter' is a good purple and 'Kentucky Wonder Wax' a striking yellow; try the first with *Clematis* 'Hagley Hybrid', the second with a double white-flowered variety.

mizuna and mustard

This pretty foliage combination from salad expert Joy Larkcom contrasts a broad-leaved red mustard, 'Red Giant', with another oriental brassica with green and fantastically cut leaves, called mizuna greens, in this case 'Mizuna Early'. Here, she has them growing close together so that they can be harvested as a cut-and-come-again salad. It is a perfect combination to use for intercropping between slower-growing crops such as beetroot: the salad leaves can be picked and eaten well before the larger crop is ready to be harvested.

Light shade and a fairly rich, moist soil will suit both plants, making them perfect for the smallest kitchen gardens, even windowbox-sized ones. They could just as easily be grown in a large tub or container. Use this planting to give fast colour to potager beds before more structural plants provide any visual impact.

There are huge numbers of mustards to choose from: gardeners in cooler areas will appreciate 'Green-in-the-Snow', which is exceptionally hardy and pale green. But don't be afraid to try crinkly-leaved sorts, mixed with red-leaved varieties of lettuce and chicory.

cultivation As the plants aren't grown to maturity, patches can be sown every few weeks through the season, starting from early spring. Sprinkle the seed thinly over finely raked soil, then firm down. Make sure you keep the soil moist at all times. Once the leaves are a few centimetres long you can harvest as much as you need. Most mustards are very hardy and prefer cool weather, tending to go to seed if the temperature rises too high. A late sowing in mid- to late-summer will give you a crop right through winter; protecting it with a cloche will keep the leaves clean.

extending the grouping The flavour of both crops can be peppery; red and green oak-leaved and other lettuces will soften the taste. A scattering of borage plants will contribute to the scheme and their blue petals look lovely in salads; likewise, a few plants of dark red nasturtium 'Indian Queen' (*Tropaeolum*), whose leaves and flowers are both edible. The whole grouping can be put to good effect between rows of ruby chard and red cabbages.

Rosemary Verey

right A rectangular bed, edged with young lettuces, is filled with red-leaved and cos varieties to make a satisfying pattern. Young leeks will grow to provide a winter crop. Use lettuces like 'Red Salad Bowl', 'Lobjoits Green Cos' or 'Goya'.

far right below The combinations on the tunnel at Barnsley House change each season, but usually incorporate a climbing variety of squash. Here, one is teamed with deep carmine sweet peas, with a luxurious planting of annual rudbeckias below.

IF THE POTAGER IS WHERE FRUIT AND VEGETABLE GROWING BECOMES elevated to an art form, then the example created by Mrs Verey and her husband at Barnsley House must rank as a masterpiece. The celebrated gardener and designer – whose clients include the Prince of Wales and Elton John – inherited the seventeenth-century house near Cirencester in Gloucestershire in 1951. From knowing only a little more than the average countrywoman about gardening, Mrs Verey became passionate about the garden. With a sharp and discerning eye, she devised for it a crisply formal layout which is strongly redolent of the seventeenth century, and filled it with exuberant and interesting combinations of plants.

The potager had been an old-fashioned vegetable patch, but under Mrs Verey's care since the early 1980s, it has become one of the garden's most famous features. Though scarcely more than 20m (215ft) square, it is exceptionally stylish both in conception and in execution. The paths are edged with low box hedges and rows of topiary balls, and basic structure is given by standard pruned roses, a 'tunnel' that in summer supports squashes and beans (and is often underplanted with rudbeckias or marigolds), and by the arbour engulfed with golden hop (the young stems can be eaten like wild asparagus in spring).

Fruit trees and some soft fruit, notably gooseberries, are pruned into fanciful shapes, but the chief glory of the kitchen garden is in Mrs Verey's original and imaginative use of vegetables, and the full exploitation of their visual possibilities. Devices such as interplanting of a bed of squat, round lettuces with spiky leeks demonstrates wit and an appreciation of the constraints of space that is hard to beat.

above Box-edged beds at Barnsley House overflow with brassicas, potatoes and beans. Rows of bread-seed poppies add gorgeous colours and, further back, the arbour is covered with golden hop.

Wildflower Meadows

above Wildflowers here set off an old yellow shrub rose to perfection. There are now increasing numbers of seed sources and businesses devoted to providing wild material, but it is best to go to a local specialist for seeds or plants descended from those in your own area.

right Cornflowers and poppies, old walls and gates, make a romantic scene. Planting wildflowers local to your part of the country means you can be sure of their suitability for the conditions; they need far less maintenance and will establish easily.

MEDIEVAL GARDENS HAD 'FLOWERY MEADS' PLANTED with grassland or meadow species, such as sweet violets, thymes, wild strawberries and grasses. They were sophisticated allusions to the wild and dangerous nature beyond the garden walls, and were meant to be places where a unicorn might – just – be tempted to graze.

Now, with the outside world generally seen as less threatening, gardeners want to re-create the vanishing wild, whether using the native flowers of the English downs or those of Texan grasslands. These days almost any wild creature that strays into the garden will seem to have something of the mythic attraction of the unicorn.

Wildflower plantings can be used in virtually any garden, not simply in meadows set aside specifically for the purpose. They can look lovely and are easy to maintain. If you want to include other styles within your garden, too, it is a good idea to keep wildflower plantings to the margins, or at least those of its cultivated areas. Alternatively, if your garden is large enough, go the whole way and take wild plants right up to the walls of your house and plant woodland flowers beneath your orchard trees. If you have space to plant tree species, the wild ones from your own terrain will work best in the wider landscape, and are just as well suited to local suburban areas and even inner cities.

However, there is no real reason why your garden, wherever it is, should not feature exotic wildflowers: a French garden with native Himalayan flowers or an American one with Australian plants, is both possible and potentially lovely. In using non-native species in your wildflower garden you would be following the precedent set by distinguished gardeners such as William Robinson (see Introduction); he often used non-native wildflowers (often American) to create his wild gardens. Having said that, the wildflowers of France and the astonishing species of North America, whether from the forests of the north or the plains of Texas and Wyoming, are so beautiful that there really is no need to plant anything but the gardener's native plants.

Ancient

Ancient civilizations were much more closely acquainted with wildflowers than we are today. Wildflowers were used in prehistoric burial ceremonies, for example, and important medicinal, magical, ritual and culinary uses were documented by 1000BC, when a Babylonian King wrote a catalogue of the vegetables, fruits and herbs in his garden. Roman emperors grew both Italian and foreign wild plants from cherries (brought to Italy from Anatolia) to dates.

Most medieval herb gardens seem to have grown many species from their local floras, with a few from foreign climes or from gardens long past. Medieval flower gardens relied on wildflowers, too; illuminated prayer books and other manuscripts commonly show wild roses, vetches, violets and daisies, familiar from contemporary hedgerows. A few show variants of wildflowers (double daisies, pinks, carnations), and such rarities were usually grown on their own.

Medieval garden meadows or flowery meads – sophisticated re-creations of wilderness on a small scale – often made use of combinations found naturally in the wild, with violets, thymes, daisies and wild strawberries amongst the grasses.

violas and campanulas

This pairing of violas and campanulas has a long history – paintings of them, along with mignonette (*Reseda odorata*) are in illuminated manuscripts such as the Warburg *Hours* in the Library of Congress, Washington D.C. The pairing is as comfortable in a medieval knot garden as in a Victorian bedding scheme. Neither plant will tolerate being shaded by more rampant neighbours, so grow them around a seat, or on a sunny, part-turfed raised bed.

There is a wide variety of each. Try violas such as *Viola cornuta* and its forms or the black-flowered annual 'Bowles' Black'. Campanulas include *C. rapunculoides*, which is large and invasive; or *C. rapunculus* for a kitchen garden – it used to be grown for its edible roots.

cultivation Both plants prefer moist but well-drained soil and will grow in sun or shade. Violas are weakly perennial, but once you have a few plants – easily grown from seed – they will self-seed in your garden. Campanulas are tough perennials and need little attention.

extending the grouping The planting shown right includes mignonette from Libya, which was grown in ancient Mediterranean gardens, but only became popular in northern Europe in the eighteenth century. Its greeny-yellow flower heads contrast with the soft blue of the campanula and the perky colours of the viola. More colourful forms of mignonette simply don't smell as sweet. It is an annual, and will need sowing afresh each season: in autumn, pot up a plant or two and take them indoors. Put them on a sunny windowsill and they'll keep flowering into midwinter and perfume the room into the bargain. Instead of mignonette, try adding wild strawberries (*Fragaria vesca*) and sweet violets (*Viola odorata*) to the combination, and you can make your own perfect 'flowery mead' in miniature. In the kitchen garden, thymes and the smaller oreganos would make companionable additions.

far left Several sorts of viola mix delightfully with white Canterbury bells (*Campanula medium* 'Calycanthema') and the ancient 'Melancoly Gentleman' (*Astrantia minor*).

left The old peach-leaved bellflower (*Campanula persicifolia*) is a good border plant, and has been in gardens since the sixteenth century. It combines marvellously with violas and old roses (in this case 'Old Blush China'). On the right is *Parahebe perfoliata*, introduced from Australia in 1834.

above The wild *Viola tricolor* with harebells (*Campanula rotundifolia*) alongside mignonette.

Traditional

Interest in the non-medicinal native flora of Europe began to expand in the early Renaissance. It was an exciting time, associated with exploration and conquest in North and Central America and trading expansion in the East, and exotic new plants began to arrive in European gardens, often to be re-exported to American ones.

A number of traditional plant combinations arose at this time, succeeded by many more in the eighteenth and early nineteenth centuries. They may have originated in a particular garden or at the hands of a particular gardener, but most information about their origins is long lost but for references in garden books of the time.

forget-me-nots and welsh poppies

Classic combinations do not have to feature rare or difficult plants: so do not let sniffy gardeners put you off this traditional pairing by saying that the plants involved are no more than weeds. The lemony-yellow Welsh poppy (*Meconopsis cambrica*) will flower for much of late spring and summer alongside the tiny, sky-blue forget-me-nots (*Myosotis* hybrids), which have only a slightly shorter season of flower. This combination was probably first used in the nineteenth century.

Plant it under fruit trees, surrounding late-season tulips or under rose bushes: I have them growing amongst old Scots roses, hybrids of *Rosa pimpinellifolia*.

cultivation Both plants grow well in partial shade, though they like good soil and reasonable moisture, and both will self-seed. The Welsh poppy is a tenacious perennial: dig it up when it strays. By late summer you will need to clear away old flowering stems. The forget-me-not is a biennial, so leave old flower stems to shed seed.

extending the grouping Add hardy ferns (such as *Dryopteris filix-mas*) and plants with linear leaves, perhaps *Iris pseudacorus* or *I. sibirica* – an indigo-blue variety would be very effective.

foxgloves and
cornflowers

Simple plantings can have great impact: the speckled purple bells of foxgloves (*Digitalis*) contrast well with the intense violet-blue of the cornflowers' (*Centaurea cyanus*) baroque thistles. The combination was popular in the eighteenth century and is perfect in a wildflower meadow, a small-scale wild garden or even a cottagey flower border.

cultivation Both plants do well in sun, though the foxglove also tolerates deep shade, and both do best in moist, but well-drained soil. The foxglove is a biennial, so will not flower in its first season, while this particular cornflower is an annual which does not self-seed easily in colder gardens – it needs to be sown every season. If you are planting into grassland, grow the young foxgloves on in pots first; for the cornflowers, clear about half a square metre (2sq ft) of turf, and sow into the fresh soil. Young plants get shaded out easily, so keep watch until they are nearly in flower.

extending the grouping Add the ordinary corn cockle and pale Shirley poppies. I would include the arching silvery leaves of *Stipa gigantea* to give some glitter, plus the purple spires of *Lythrum salicaria*, as well as some wild valerian (*Centranthus ruber*).

violas and
erythroniums

The wildflowers *Erythronium revolutum* and *Viola biflora* make a harmonious traditional combination from America, matching the elegant upswept petals of the erythronium with the flowers of the violet. William Robinson advocated similar plantings. A bonus is that the foliage of both contrast well in scale, colour and markings. European gardeners could use the equally pretty *Erythronium denscanis* and *Viola odorata* or the part-yellow *V. tricolor* in their gardens.

It is a perfect combination for a woodland garden, for the margins of a shrub rose border or under hazels in a nuttery, and it also works well in a small urban garden under flowering cherry or peach trees.

cultivation The erythronium is a bulb that establishes easily and, once it does, it should self-sow happily. The viola is simply grown from seed. Both plants like shade and a rich soil with plenty of leafmould.

extending the grouping Cardamines, particularly the soft cream *Cardamine enneaphyllos*, and the double form of *Sanguinaria canadensis*, with brilliant white flowers and blue-grey foliage, will complement the planting. Try them all beneath clumps of paeonies; I use pale yellow *Paeonia mlokosewitschii* but any will look good.

previous pages The lemon-yellow of the Welsh poppy and sky-blue of the forget-me-not make a stunning display as a ground cover planting in a tiny urban garden or yard.

far left Foxglove species are becoming increasingly fashionable, with breeders producing strains like 'Sutton's Apricot', or the plain white form. If you would rather have a perennial cornflower, *Centaurea dealbata* (violet-mauve) or the fine pale yellow *C. ruthenica* might fit the bill.

left There are many *Erythronium* hybrids; this one is *E. revolutum*, but you could choose the yellow *E.* 'Pagoda'. Instead of *Viola biflora*, try *V. sororia*: the form 'Freckles' is splashed in two shades of violet.

Designer

After 1800 the influx into European gardens of native American flowers was so great that they became almost the main constituents of herbaceous borders. Similarly, American trees and shrubs dominated the arboretum and shrubbery. Designers and gardeners took up the new introductions with enthusiasm, increasingly so when European nurserymen started producing glamorous garden forms.

William Robinson (see Introduction) thought that many of them were perfect for his proposed 'wild garden', which put wildflowers together in a naturalistic way, and not in the formal borders or bedding arrangements that he so hated. However, his wild garden happily contained species from North America, China and Afghanistan. He gave little thought to 'local' authenticity, even though his style was taken up by Arts and Crafts devotees, concerned with authentically vernacular 'English' houses, furnishings and lifestyles.

Since Robinson's time, 'authenticity' in the garden has come to mean antique plants around antique houses, or local plants for local gardens. It is now possible to buy wildflower seed (or plants grown from it) harvested from meadows and woodland in your own area.

Over the past decade or so wildflower planting has become a widespread and important theme in gardening. It is especially strong in geographic areas with rich floras, especially North America and mainland Europe and many of today's designers, from Christopher Lloyd to Piet Oudolf, use wild plants in consciously decorative ways, often creating novel plant groups.

Try not to be too dogmatic about the species you use. Follow the example of William Robinson and of many European designers: if you garden in Europe, use good American plants like *Echinacea purpurea* or *Lupinus polyphyllus*. Many American designers use Japanese bamboos or European loosestrifes. Experiment and have fun; it is an exciting moment in the evolution of gardening.

linaria and centranthus

These plants are both European wildflowers, but they seem only to have been encouraged into the garden by nineteenth-century designers seeking a rather wild and romantic look. William Robinson, in particular, popularized this combination of scarlet valerian

right The common yellow toadflax, *Linaria vulgaris*, is a cheerful plant that will do well in borders. If you want something a little more special, look for *L. dalmatica*, which has similar flowers but finely divided blue-green leaves that would partner white valerian.

far right The colours are marvellous, but remember that both linaria and centranthus have tough and penetrating roots that will gradually prise apart the stones between which they grow. Don't let either get established on valuable masonry, especially the valerian, whose seed is equipped with airy 'parachutes' that let them travel with ease into the highest nooks and crannies.

(*Centranthus ruber*) and *Linaria purpurea* when he used it to soften the steps and balustrades at Gravetye in Kent. You can grow them just as William Robinson did or you can plant them in an open border. The valerian has a mild perfume and bees love the linaria, so they make a pleasant planting around a seat or at the base of a wall where the soil is poor and little else will grow.

Valerian has, even in the wild, a colour range from deep brick-scarlets, through pinks, to pure white. Seedlings from a single plant can span the range, though white is often the most popular amongst gardeners. *Linaria purpurea* has a pink variant called 'Canon Went' and a lavender-blue hybrid called 'Yuppie Surprise'. Do explore the many hybrid strains, especially *L. maroccana* 'Fairy Bouquet'. Many will self-seed themselves in paving and gravel, making an attractive

display. Some of the species, especially *L. dalmatica* and *L. vulgaris*, are perennials that can be invasive, but do still try them amongst valerians and artemisias.

cultivation Valerian and linaria like sun and will grow in the most barren soil provided their long tap roots can reach some moisture and nourishment. Both seed themselves widely – the linaria with particular abandon – so you will soon have plenty of plants to experiment with.

extending the grouping Plants that grow in dry crevices make good companions. Try some of the sisyrinchiums, ideally *S. striatum*, with grey-green leaves and cream flowers. Some of the rock-garden dianthus would be excellent, too, as well as *D.* 'Loveliness', with strange feathered flowers and a sweet smell.

flax and geraniums

In this combination from the designer Urs Walser in Hermannshof in Germany, the sky-blue of the flax (*Linum perenne*) is complemented by the amethyst-purple of the cranesbill (*Geranium sanguineum*). The leaves work together, too: blue-green and narrow in the flax and veined and palmate in the cranesbill.

cultivation Both plants are perennial. The flax is easily grown from seed; you may find it more convenient to buy the geranium as plants. Both are hardy and prefer good soil, and both will tolerate shade.

extending the grouping The planting shown left includes St Bruno's lily (*Paradisea liliastrum*), whose white flowers set off the combination. This combination could follow on from the foxgloves and cornflowers on page 95; add some shrubs, perhaps hydrangeas like *H. villosa* and *H.* 'Preziosa', for late-season accent.

geraniums and salvias

Some gardeners think cerise is a terrible colour in the garden, but in the guise of *Geranium psilostemon* it makes an irreproachable combination with the toning hues of clary (*Salvia sclarea turkestanica*). Both were popular in the late nineteenth century. There are satisfying contrasts in the foliage, too, between the large clary leaves and palmately cut cranesbill. There are many salvias to choose from: try *Salvia involucrata* with its furry cerise bracts.

cultivation Clary is a biennial, though occasionally plants do last for several seasons The cranesbill shown is a hybrid and must be bought ready grown. Both tolerate shade and poor soil.

extending the grouping In the planting shown left, the silvery-pink of musk mallow (*Malva moschata*) sets off the combination. The large bracts of the clary have a blue tinge that is set off by blue campanulas: *Campanula persicifolia* is one of the easiest to grow.

ceanothus and
fremontodendron

Widely used in the 1920s, this full-blooded colour scheme, combining two Californian plants, has become a classic in mild gardens in Europe and America. The silvery-blue of the ceanothus complements the brick-yellow of the fremontodendron, and both tones are subtler than the more usual cold-garden summer pairing of lilac and laburnum.

The pairing is ideal for sunny urban gardens where winter temperatures do not drop too low. It looks splendid around a summerhouse, accompanied by low-maintenance annuals.

Fremontodendron is a small genus; only one species is much used – *F. californicum* – whose hybrid 'California Glory' has slightly grander flowers. However, there are hundreds of *Ceanothus* variants, with flower colours ranging from acid and chilly pinks to deep violet-blues. The pale blue *C.* x *delileanus* 'Gloire de Versailles' is easy to grow.

cultivation Both genera like full sun and poor soils. Fertile soil is to be avoided because it promotes lush growth, which is less winter hardy. Both also like to be planted young, for their roots resent disturbance. Though there are many hybrids of ceanothus, the larger ones that match the scale of the fremontodendron will eventually need pruning, which should be done in early spring. If you need to prune the fremontodendron into shape, avoid inhaling the fuzz from the stems or getting it in your eyes as it can cause irritation. Neither genus is long-lived, but both are easily propagated from cuttings.

extending the grouping You could add contrast by putting a large white clematis through the pair, though I would choose something silvery for later in the season, such as *C. flammula* with its sheaves of white perfumed flowers, or *C.* x *jouiniana*. Alternatively, extend the scheme with roses such as 'Lawrence Johnston' or 'Alister Stella Gray'. Best of all ideas is to plant the combination against a sunny wall with *Rosa banksiae* and jasmine.

centranthus and erigeron

Erigeron and wild valerian (*Centranthus ruber*) look wonderful planted on either side of a flight of steps at Park Farm in Essex. *Erigeron karvinskianus* (often still called *E. mucronatus*), the most popular erigeron, arrived from Mexico in 1836. It was taken up later in the century by wild garden enthusiasts, and has become naturalized in parts of south-west Britain, the Channel Islands and southern Europe.

Erigeron will also colonize terrraces and the cracks between patio paving if these are not sealed with concrete. It establishes well on gravel drives and forecourts, where it softens the bleakness that these areas sometimes have. It is far happier there than in the open border.

There are a number of interesting erigerons for the garden. Try *E. philadelphicus* (which arrived from North America in 1778) amongst stonework. It is taller than *E. karvinskianus* and has clusters of clearer pink daisy flowers. Or add drama with the intense violet-blue flowers of *E. macranthus*, which came from the Rocky Mountains in 1841. Many of the most popular erigerons are selections and hybrids of *E. speciosus* from western North America. They include 'Superbus' of 1889 and 'Quakeress' and 'White Quakeress' of the 1890s.

cultivation Both plants like full sun. In colder gardens, the erigeron is difficult to establish – I know, I've tried hard enough in mine. The trick is to keep a few plants growing in a pot and overwinter them in a sheltered spot. In warmer gardens, once you have a few plants, which are easily grown from seed, they will soon start spreading with abandon. Erigeron does well in retaining walls and rockeries, though doesn't generally get established in solid masonry. Unlike deep-rooted valerian, plants are easily pulled up if they are in the wrong place. For more details on centranthus see page 96.

extending the grouping On walls, add the little ivy-leaved toadflax (*Cymbalaria muralis*), especially if you can find the pure white form. On steps, plant some germanders: *Teucrium fruticans* has some nice wavy-edged leaf forms. If the steps have damp soil beneath, the yellow-green flowers of *Alchemilla mollis* make an excellent foil for both erigeron and centranthus.

brunnera and
hogweed

There is some dangerous greenery here, yet what gardener can fail to be impressed by the foliage of the giant hogweed (*Heracleum mantegazzianum*) or its huge flower and seed heads? In this combination, the vast biennial is planted in a sea of the perennial forget-me-not, *Brunnera macrophylla*, which itself has attractive foliage, plus airy drifts of blue flowers from early spring to the start of summer. Many designers have used the hogweed, first advocated by William Robinson but admired by Gertrude Jekyll, too.

Grand wild gardens are perfect for this planting, but they must be gardens where children won't crash through the undergrowth and not acres where neglect reigns. In some areas, hogweed is forbidden, so check before you buy.

Variants of the brunnera include *B. macrophylla* 'Langtrees', with a handsome ring of silver spots on the leaves. There are other heracleums, though none have as dramatic leaves as this.

cultivation Both species will cope with deep shade, given plenty of moisture and rich soil. The juice from giant hogweed stems and petioles can cause severe and long-lasting blistering on sensitive skin. Try to avoid all contact with the juice, and wash it off immediately in case of accidental exposure; sunshine on contaminated skin exacerbates the problem. Hogweed self-seeds so prolifically that it can easily invade large areas of ground, particularly along river banks. In addition the seed can lie dormant in the soil for several seasons. Be ruthless in dealing with the seedlings: use weedkiller, not the hoe, and never use a strimmer, which sprays the juice everywhere. On a gentler note, brunnera makes clumps that are easily divided in spring though the plants in my garden self-seed prolifically. All brunnera seed more or less true.

extending the grouping Here, the basic planting is augmented with the grass *Phalaris arundinacea* in its variegated form known as gardeners garters. Archangel (*Lamium galeobdolon*) and other thugs complete the picture. If you really cannot face using hogweed, angelica (*Angelica archangelica*) can be almost as dramatic.

far left *Erigeron karvinskianus* flowers for most of its growing season and seeds enthusiastically in milder gardens. Here, the gardener has been hoeing a clear ascent. The valerian flowers for much of the summer; it can be cut back once or twice during the season to ensure generous amounts of colour.
left No garden plant has quite the drama of the Caucasian giant hogweed.

grasses and sedges

New interest in the decorative possibilities of grasses, sedges and related plants has led to some spectacularly different combinations, many now on their way to 'classic' status. Though selected grasses have been used in borders since the seventeenth century, and many were popular late nineteenth-century garden plants (pampas grass particularly), modern designers like Piet Oudolf, working mainly in Europe, and Wolfgang Oehme and James Van Sweden in America, have exploited their potential to the full.

The huge number of species available were largely ignored in the past because they are not conventionally 'colourful', yet the way their inflorescences catch the light is almost as important as their basic colour. They also bring texture and movement into planting schemes, qualities that are increasingly valued in contemporary design.

Obviously, grasses have strong associations with the meadows, fields and prairies of the wider landscape and are good for giving the garden a softer, more naturalistic look. The elegance of the foliage combines dramatically with broad-leaved flowers and ferns, but the subtle colouring of grasses has itself been exploited, too, particularly by American designers like George Hargreaves and the Englishman Dan Pearson, whose planting schemes are able skilfully to utilize their bleached-out tones.

Plantings that use just grasses and sedges are most successful if the foliage or flower spikes are carefully contrasted, and if they are planted in large enough quantities to make clear the subtle differences between them. They are most suitable for large areas, especially around modern buildings – particularly those with large, smooth, neutral-coloured surfaces. Modern designers like Oehme and van Sweden build up layers of grasses, such as pennisetums, calamagrostis and miscanthus, which they plant in broad sweeps to follow the undulations of the landscape or the line of a pool edge. There is an art in combining species that manage to complement each other without competing for attention. To discover more about grasses, it is worth studying their individual characteristics in the grass collections of a botanic garden.

Grasses also include the exciting bamboo family, where plants of all sizes can be found, from useful ground-covers to species with great structural impact. In modern surroundings or in sheltered yards, small and medium-sized forms can make the perfect contrast to architecture. Species like the broad-leaved *Sasa veitchii* look stunning against a plain wall (perhaps underplanted with *Vinca minor*, or ferns and mosses); equally striking would be the sombre-stemmed *Phyllostachys nigra* with *Brunnera macrophylla* 'Langtrees'. Many species of grass and sedge look good in early spring and provide a useful foil in the summer border, reaching their peak in autumn.

cultivation Grasses and sedges can be found in many habitats, from dry and open prairie to shady water margins. Most of those in cultivation will grow in ordinary soil with average moisture, and many bamboos actually prefer the shelter of buildings or woodland. Because the geographical range of the group is so wide, check before purchasing a particular plant that it will be hardy in your area.

Many grasses and sedges are invasive, and plantings need regular and careful maintenance to keep the division between them clear. Creeping species should be checked regularly or planted amongst strong-growing shrubs, which will help to shade them out and will compete with over-vigorous growth.

The invasiveness of grasses sets this type of planting apart from another element in modern gardening, the meadow. There, maintenance is kept to a minimum, and the grasses and other plants used are capable of withstanding mowing several times a year, but none of the species described here will tolerate heavy cutting.

extending the grouping Grasses and sedges can also be combined with herbaceous plants, their linear leaves offering fine contrasts to bold foliage. *Miscanthus sinensis* with ligularias, *Stipa gigantea* with *Rudbeckia* 'Herbstsonne', *Pennisetum villosum* with *Lysimachia atropurpurea*, *Panicum clandestinum* with bergenias as a planting beneath mauve-red roses (perhaps 'Roseraie de l'Haÿ'), or *Carex elata* 'Aurea' and *Rodgersia aesculifolia* by the pool edge, are just a few of the myriad possibilities. Be sure to choose plants with the same cultural needs as your grasses, grouping together water-loving species or those that like dry, open conditions.

above left
Tall *Miscanthus floridulus* backs bands of *Calamagrostis* x *acutiflora* 'Karl Foerster' and the feathery heads of *Pennisetum villosum*. Contrast is provided by the dull purple flowers of *Eupatorium purpureum*.
centre left The late-summer flower spikes of *Calamagrostis* x *acutiflora* 'Karl Foerster' combine well with *Echinacea purpurea* 'Magnus', though the ivory-green form 'White Swan' would look good too.
below left
Carex muskingumensis 'Oehme', with its chestnut seed-heads, is here contrasted with *Sparganium erectum*, in front of a bank of grass seed-heads. The sparganium needs damp ground in order for it to flourish.

right Camassias from North America – easily naturalized in meadows – alliums and drifts of narcissi make an attractive sight beneath a young oak tree at Great Dixter. This combination would look equally good beneath orchard trees.

far right above Wild orchids along with goatsbeards *(Tragopogon pratensis)* make a gorgeous show against the light; orchids like *Dactylorhiza maculata* and others are now easily available and are not taken from the wild.

CHRISTOPHER LLOYD WAS BORN IN 1921, AND GREW UP IN HIS FAMILY home, Great Dixter in Sussex, England. The ancient timber-framed house, much of it fifteenth century, had a splendid garden created by his parents, which first opened to the public in 1929. The gardens and plants fascinated him as a child, an interest much encouraged by his parents. He took a degree in horticulture in 1950 and, after a spell lecturing, returned to Great Dixter to look after the gardens and start a nursery specializing in interesting plants.

Then began his series of sharp-eyed and witty garden books and a long-running column in the influential magazine *Country Life*. With his immense knowledge and strong likes and dislikes, Christopher Lloyd's work became, and remains, much admired. His idiosyncratic approach to plants is apparent in the plant associations he creates in the gardens at Great Dixter, where you can find combinations like *Rosa glauca* teamed with *Hydrangea macrophylla* 'Générale Comtesse de Vibraye', and underplanted with *Astilbe taquetii*, and the deep-purple leaved form of *Perilla*.

However, it is his enchanting meadow, filled with fritillaries, cowslips and wild orchids that has opened many gardeners' eyes to the myriad visual possibilities of the European flora. Although other areas of Great Dixter, like the sunken garden for example, are very beautiful, the meadow will perhaps be seen to be the most influential of all the garden's many components.

Christopher Lloyd has a wide circle of gardening friends, yet has only rarely advised on other gardens: Great Dixter really is his major work. It proves that one strongly imagined space can easily have influence worldwide.

left Goatsbeard and ox-eye daisies (*Leucanthemum vulgare*) bring drama and colour to the flowering grasses. A mown path is wide enough to keep the way clear of wet foliage on a rainy day.

Cottage
Borders

above In a 'cottage' planting romantic lushness is all; here, a late-summer tangle combines verbascums, montbretias and lilies to give a feel of simple luxury. The buttressed wall suggests more of a 'country house' than a 'cottage'.

right This colourful border is a palette of pale mauve phloxes and erigerons, blue-green nigella, brilliant blue salvias, roses and campanulas with a touch of yellow for contrast. Such a colour mix can easily be scaled down for small spaces.

COTTAGE GARDENING IS OFTEN SEEN AS HARKING BACK to a vanished golden age of simplicity with no relevance to gardening today. But the tradition of cottage gardening cannot be written off so easily – it remains the source and inspiration for many successful planting combinations.

Most gardening nations have an identifiable style, in that there are Italian, French or Dutch gardens, which are adaptable to small spaces. Few British gardeners feel nostalgic for the great landscape gardens of the mid-1700s, and rarely have room to reproduce them. Their recourse is to create cottage gardens in nineteenth-century styles (particularly the various sorts of 'bedding' such as the wallflowers and tulips on pages 113–15), or to look further into the past and plant an idealized version of a farmhouse garden from a less specific era – perhaps using marigolds, nasturtiums and aquilegias.

In America, with its astonishing cultural diversity, nostalgia is perhaps harder work, though the recent formation of the American Cottage Garden Society indicates the considerable interest in this style of gardening. Certainly, at the very end of the 1800s there was much affection for the old homestead gardens, and sadness at the loss of many of them as America gradually became an industrial giant.

Whatever their origin, cottage gardens abound in France, Holland, Germany and increasingly in North America. Their very flexibility means that they present endless possibilities. In this chapter there are some combinations that look wonderful in their own right; take them towards wildflower gardening and you have a planting that suits the most modern of houses; take them towards the kitchen garden and they can make a tin shack look like an arbour in Eden.

In idealized cottage gardens, the plants are arranged rather haphazardly. Staking is kept to a minimum to increase the feeling of generous tangle, and self-sown seedlings are encouraged. Real-life cottage gardens have to cope with children, chickens, rusting wheelbarrows and much more. However, if your plants are chosen with this in mind, they can still be highly rewarding.

Ancient

Cottage gardens emerge from the shadows of history late in the day. Only oblique references to them exist before the Renaissance, and even after 1550, with that movement well underway, they are only hinted at in the more personal of the great herbals by John Gerard and John Parkinson. Unlike modern cottage gardens, with their emphasis on drifts of colour, it is very likely plants were placed singly, with care taken to ensure that no two similar species were placed next to one another. This system applied with increasing complexity of repetition well into the eighteenth century, and survived even into the 1800s as 'the promiscuous or mixed border'.

hesperis and aquilegias

These two ancient garden plants make a perfect mix: the soft strawberry-pink of the delicately shaped aquilegia (a red form of *Aquilegia vulgaris*) and the slightly violet-tinged white of sweet rocket (*Hesperis matronalis*), which also has a fine perfume. The planting, which is certainly late medieval, makes an ideal groundwork amongst bushes of antique roses, and looks pretty around a gate or at the base of an old wall. Try it, too, by the paths in an orchard.

cultivation Both plants do well in light shade and medium soil, but are happy in sun. Sweet rocket is a biennial, flowering in its second season, then dying. It is easy from seed and will self-sow once established. Some gardeners stake the flowers of sweet rocket, but in this pairing it is unnecessary as the planting depends on a loose-flowered charm. Aquilegias are perennial, and seed themselves with abandon. They are poisonous so be careful where you plant them.

extending the grouping Add any of the forms of the peach-leaved bellflower (*Campanula persicifolia*), the linear foliage of *Iris sibirica*, clumps of a perennial cornflower such as *Centaurea dealbata*, and some tall hollyhocks (*Althaea*) to give some height.

far left The hesperis (once called 'dame's violet') also comes in pale shades of mauve which combine well with aquilegias, particularly the myriad shades of blue aquilegias that are available.
left This form of *Campanula persicifolia* has pale blue margins to the bells. There are modern names for similar things, but once you have the original blue-and-white singles, you will soon find seedlings as elegant as the plant here. Look, too, for the doubles – all are good and easily grown cottage flowers from the seventeenth century.

poppies and
campanulas

The blue or white flowers of the peach-leaved bellflower (*Campanula persicifolia*) make a fine, cool contrast to the extraordinary Oriental poppy (*Papaver orientale*). Both are ancient garden plants, the poppy having been introduced from Constantinople around 1550. The combination is probably early seventeenth century.

Some gardeners find the flamboyance of the poppy tolerable in a small area only; others cannot get enough of it. For a subtle effect, position this planting against old stone walls – the red of the poppy can fight with the colour of some types of brick – or site it by an old wooden fence. Or you could opt for a different colour scheme entirely

as the poppy now comes in white and pinks, some of which have double flowers. 'Sultana' and 'Turkish Delight' are in shades of strawberry and 'Cedric Morris' is pinkish grey. All three complement grasses and deep maroon roses. The campanula has double forms including hose-in-hose sorts, where each flower contains another.

cultivation Both plants are perennials. They like good soil, tolerate shade, and are very hardy. The campanula will seed itself and make slowly expanding clumps. Some forms of the poppy have creeping rhizomes, but most make dense clumps from which you can take root cuttings in early spring. Poppies are easily grown from seed.
extending the grouping *Iris* 'Florentina', the blue *Iris germanica*, and bushes of lad's love (*Artemisia abrotanum*) and lavender will all contribute appropriately cool silver and blue tones.

Traditional

The traditional cottage garden dates back to the closing years of the eighteenth century, when landowners built for themselves, or their tenants, pretty cottages to embellish the landscape, examples of which can be found over most of Europe. Picturesque cottages needed gardens to match, filled with roses, lavender and doves, rather than a real cottage garden populated by carrots, cabbages and a pig. A number of conventional plantings arose as a result, from honeysuckle and jasmine around the porch, to the monthly roses and biennial campanulas by the front gate.

cosmos and marigolds

While marigolds (*Calendula officinalis*) have been in gardens since time immemorial, the cosmos, an annual from central America, has only been grown since the middle of the 1800s. Along with many other American annuals, it became popular because it was quick to flower after the spring bedding had been pulled. Prosperous gardeners used geraniums (now *Pelargonium*) overwintered in their greenhouses for this purpose; poorer gardeners had to make do with these fast-growing annuals – and probably had a lot more fun.

There is an extraordinary cosmos (*C. atrosanguineus*) that has deep chocolate-violet flowers with a strong chocolate scent. It likes an open border in warm gardens – try it with *Calendula* 'Art Shades'.

above Cosmos and marigolds could easily follow a spring bedding scheme of tulips and wallflowers, as they suit a similar situation.

far right and overleaf, left to right The traditional combination of tulips and wallflowers is not only suitable for bedding schemes. Try it in large containers, perhaps big square pots, on a patio or terrace. Wallflowers and some tulips are very fragrant, so put them where you can sit beside them on a warm spring morning.

cultivation Sow both sorts of seed in situ. Either broadcast the seed by hand and rake gently, then firm the soil, or draw shallow drills with a trowel, then sow the seed thinly along each drill. In either case, thin seedlings soon after germination to leave a plant every 20–30cm (8–12in). Both species like rich, moist soil and full sun.

extending the grouping The colours can be toned down by the addition of pale lemon-yellow from other cultivars of marigold, or short-growing forms of sunflower (*Helianthus annuus*) or zinnia.

tulips and wallflowers

Tulips (*Tulipa*) and wallflowers (forms of *Erysimum cheiri*) are such a familiar sight in municipal parks that it is easy to overlook how their combinations of colour and form bring late spring alive.

Both are old garden plants (tulips arrived in Europe from Constantinople in the sixteenth century; wallflowers have been a favoured garden flower for much longer), but this sort of bedding is a nineteenth-century model, popular from around 1830. It was often used as a decoration for small front gardens, usually in a bed cut out of the lawn. The success of the planting depends on being able to find colour strains or named varieties of wallflower; colour mixtures merely look messy. Tulips are sold almost entirely by variety and, as there are hundreds of these, and a couple of dozen shades of wallflower, the number of permutations is immense.

Some perennial wallflowers make low bushes, which flower in spring and summer: *Erysimum* 'Bowles' Mauve' kept trimmed works well with bronze or deep red tulips, while the pale *Erysimum* 'Moonlight' is the perfect foil to a double white tulip.

cultivation Both plants like full sun, or only light shade, and reasonable soil. Most wallflowers are biennial, flowering in their second season. Although they do not actually die after flowering, the plants are usually thrown away once the tulips have finished. This makes the whole scheme rather labour intensive, for the wallflower seed has to be sown the summer before, and the seedlings kept in nursery rows until autumn. Finally, they can be moved into position when the tulip bulbs are planted in autumn.

Once the tulips have finished flowering, they can be heeled in elsewhere in the garden until the foliage dies away in mid-summer. Then you can lift the bulbs, dry them off and store them in a dry place until autumn. Replant large bulbs in the bedding area; smaller ones can be set out elsewhere and grown on for the following season.

extending the grouping Forget-me-nots (*Myosotis*) are traditional accompaniments, giving an ethereal haze of blue amongst the planting. Use clumps of *Omphalodes cappadocica* to similar effect.

far left above
Yarrow and clary
would look good
beside a path.
far left below
The bread-seed poppy
complements the
colour scheme.
left Crambe needs
space; its flower
sprays can reach
1.8–2.2m (6–7ft) high
and across. Try the
combination in beds
under an avenue of
old apple trees.

achillea and *salvia*

The annual clary (*Salvia viridis*), grown at least since medieval times, and the equally venerable yarrow (*Achillea*) make an enchanting mix of mauve and pink for a traditional cottage garden. The planting can be arranged as a broad sward, though as it has a short flowering season, it needs something extra to give interest early and late in the year. It can also be planted in a parterre outlined in clipped lavender or box. The range of yarrows is increasing all the time, with new tones of bronze, orange and some subtle reds being bred.

cultivation Clary is an annual, best sown directly in open ground in mid-spring. Yarrow is a perennial best increased by division. Both species like sun and good soil, but will tolerate dry conditions.

extending the grouping The bread-seed poppy (*Papaver somniferum*) reinforces the colour scheme. Or add something greyer, but in the same colour range, such as *Salvia sclarea* var. *turkestanica*, with big leaves and dramatic purple bracts. Adding *S.* x *superba* 'Superba' tips the colour balance towards blue, and asters and Japanese anemones keep the colour theme going later in the season.

delphiniums and *crambe*

Not all cottage garden plants are small; this combination (dating from the late nineteenth century) uses two giants – delphiniums and the enormous *Crambe cordifolia*. The blue and purple spires of the delphinium are brilliantly offset by clouds of tiny white crambe flowers in early summer. These smell very sweetly of honey, but are too overpowering to cut for the house.

cultivation Crambe and delphiniums are easily grown perennials. Crambe is increased by seed or by taking root cuttings. Delphiniums can be grown from seed or bought as named plants. You can then propagate them by treating some of the shoots produced in spring as cuttings: when they are 15cm (6in) long, slice them off as close to the root-stock as you can and pot them on until ready to plant out.

Both plants like rich soil and tolerate light shade. Only the delphiniums need staking. Watch out for caterpillars and slugs.

extending the grouping Try some irises in the foreground, like the heavily perfumed and soft blue *Iris pallida*, or its variegated forms. Some of the big bearded irises would be good, too.

Designer

Naturally, nineteenth-century garden writers and designers made use of both the new flora and old-fashioned cottage plants in colour schemes suitable for their readers. Rather like today, magazines and books were aimed at all sections of the reading market, from the most exclusive to the most humble. And from the vast resources of Victorian gardening, dozens of designer-based combinations survive, some still widely used, others more than worth reviving. The Victorian painter and flower arranger Frances Hope used ancient double wallflowers and lilies just introduced from China, and Gertrude Jekyll filled the cottage borders at Munstead Wood with brand new hybrid lupins and delphiniums (a combination often thought of as 'traditional', but not possible before 1900 or so). Even Margery Fish liked and planted at least some species introduced in the 1920s.

Contemporary cottages, however, are actually more common in North America, where ownership of a modern summer home, whether a modest cabin or a sophisticated house, but with a piece of land for vegetables, fruit and flowers, is more common than in Europe. Nevertheless, both European and American designers are producing lovely modern plantings for cottage gardens.

love-in-a-mist and alliums

The pairing of blue love-in-a-mist (*Nigella damascena*) and alliums makes an alluring planting – the onion flowers creating purple sparks amongst the haze of nigella foliage. The basic species of nigella has been grown at least since medieval times, while the allium is a nineteenth-century introduction. This nigella is the form called 'Miss Jekyll', and was developed at Munstead Wood. Gertrude Jekyll also liked alliums and this seems to be one of her 'cottagey' combinations.

The overall height of this plant combination is low, so site it under fruit or nut trees, as the mauve-blue part of a Jekyll-style border, or as a base-planting amongst grey-pink shrub roses.

There is a large range of nigellas from which to choose, varying in colour from white to dark blue. The number of alliums is legion, but the deep smoky-blue *Allium caeruleum* will complement either white or dark blue nigellas.

cultivation The nigella is annual, and needs sowing in spring where it is to flower. It could not be easier: just broadcast the seed and rake in gently. The allium is a good hardy bulb, but its leaves sprout early, so be careful not to damage them when sowing the nigella. Both like sun or light shade, and will tolerate average or poor soil. If left to their own devices, both plants will self-sow, so you may have to be ruthless in pulling up unwanted seedlings.

extending the grouping Add agapanthus if your garden is large enough to support their size, and bright sparks of mauve-red *Gladiolus communis* ssp. *byzantinus*. Any of the green-yellow flowered euphorbias such as *Euphorbia palustris* make a good addition: back the whole combination with hebes, or *Rosa moyesii* mixed with *Rosa glauca*.

achillea and verbascum

The horizontal yellow heads of *Achillea filipendulina* are contrasted with the grey-pink vertical spikes of a modern hybrid verbascum. This is a perfect combination for a dryish, sunny border around a patio, or along the path to your front door.

cultivation The achillea is a stout perennial, and needs little care except division of the clumps to avoid overcrowding after three or four seasons' growth. The verbascum is a short-lived perennial, like its parent *V. phoeniceum*. Named forms like *V. chaixii* 'Pink Domino' need to be propagated from root cuttings, though *V. phoeniceum* is easily grown from seed, producing pink and purple flowers.
extending the grouping Add pale yellow or rusty-brown spires from *Digitalis grandiflora* and *D. ferruginea* towards the front of the planting, along with a clear rose-pink (*Physostegia virginiana*) set amongst the basic pair.

globe thistle and gypsophila

The beefy metallic-blue spheres of the globe thistle (*Echinops ritro*), contrast sharply with the somewhat airy and insubstantial flower sprays of baby's breath (*Gypsophila paniculata*). The combination makes a startling basis for a sophisticated cottage border; equally, its restrained colours mean that it is suitable for a meditative space in almost any garden.

cultivation The globe thistle is a hardy perennial, easily grown from seed, though best bought as a named variety: gypsophila can be treated as an annual or bought as grafted plants. Both appreciate good soil and sun but will tolerate poor soils and some shade.
extending the grouping The vast jagged leaves and flower spikes of *Acanthus mollis* add contrast. Some herbaceous clematis species, such as *C. hendersonii*, have blue flowers that add a crisp note.

echinacea and
cimicifuga

Pink *Echinacea purpurea*, much used by modern designers, is cleverly contrasted with the reddish-leaved and spire-shaped flowers of the cimicifuga. Both are late-summer flowering, making a smooth transition into the splendours of autumn. There are a number of echinaceas to choose from: *E. purpurea* 'Magnus' is deep purple; 'White Swan' is a marvellous shade of ivory. Most cimicifugas are taller than *E. purpurea*, and should be planted behind the echinacea.

cultivation Both plants are hardy perennials and prefer rich, moist soil and full sun. Both will tolerate shade, but the echinacea is short-lived in cool, damp gardens. It can be easily raised from seed, but the biggest and best-coloured flowers come from named divisions. Cimicifuga can be grown from seed sown in autumn.

extending the grouping *Lysimachia clethroides* in front of the combination adds a bit of extra oomph as shown. If the border is shaded, add pulmonarias and brunneras.

achillea and
salvia

A favourite combination of Graham Stuart Thomas, this pairing of *Achillea filipendulina* 'Gold Plate' and *Salvia* x *superba* 'Superba' (overleaf) mixes mustard-yellow horizontals with the vertical tiers of mauve salvia flowers. It is an easy combination for a sunny border, wrapped in big drifts around a modern house, or along a path. If you want less height, use *S. nemorosa* 'East Friesland' combined with another achillea, such as *A.* 'Coronation Gold'.

cultivation Both plants are stout perennials, happy in dryish, fertile soil. Both are easily propagated by division.

extending the grouping Add a silvery artemisia such as *A.* 'Silver Queen', with cerise *Potentilla nepalensis* 'Miss Willmott'. Clumps of sunflower 'Italian White' or 'Moonwalker' can be planted at the back.

top Verbascums often have dramatically coloured anthers, creating a subtle look to the flowers. It is a genus worth exploring by every cottage gardener. Achillea, too, is a variable group, and it is possible to create many attractive combinations between the genera.

centre The globes of the thistle are made up of tightly packed cones of bracts, from each of which emerges a pale blue flower – intricate marvels that repay a closer look.

bottom A chic planting of echinacea and cimicifuga suits a sophisticated site: in a front garden or beside a path.

overleaf The dark background is a perfect foil to the combination of achillea and salvia; a dark-painted fence or an ivy-covered wall would do just as well. Both plants grow in dry soil, making an ideal pairing at the base of hedges.

eryngium and
campanula

The simplicity of the campanula makes a pleasing counterpoint to the complexity of the eryngium in a combination popular with many gardeners, among them the Irish gardener Helen Dillon, who grows it among other plants which demand the same conditions. The combination has many permutations. A particularly good one combines *Eryngium alpinum*, with its spiny bracts (which was known in Elizabethan gardens, but hardly grown until the late 1800s) with *Campanula persicifolia* (which has almost the status of a weed in its usual blue form). This produces a combination that is very Jekyll-esque in its mixing of the simple and the rare, and demonstrates the versatility of the pairing.

The planting would suit a paved area surrounding an old sundial, particularly if you added pots of sharp pink geraniums; alternatively try it along a rustic path in an orchard.

There are many eryngiums in cultivation: *Eryngium giganteum* is a biennial species no garden should be without, having huge bony ruffs that last into winter; *E. planum* has many lovely cultivars. *Campanula persicifolia* is the only campanula of its size with such airy grace, but *C. lactiflora* can also partner this eryngium successfully.

cultivation These are tough and easy-going perennials, producing more flowers in sun and poor soil. The eryngium is slow to increase, so you may want to harvest seed from the heads once they turn brown. Sow the seed immediately and leave outdoors to overwinter. Grow the young plants on in a nursery row for a season or so before planting out. You might want, eventually, to stop the campanula from seeding so prolifically. When cutting off the flower stalks, beware of the white juice, which can be hard to get off if it dries on your skin.

extending the grouping A backdrop of purple delphiniums, deep blue bearded irises and some *Acanthus spinosus*, with its large and glossy leaves contribute structure and even more glitter. I have a planting like this around bushes of the old rose 'Ispahan'.

foxglove and cupid's dart

This smart planting mixes the rich strawberry-pink of the hybrid foxglove *Digitalis* x *mertonensis* with the serene blue of cupid's dart (*Catananche caerulea*). The foxglove has larger flowers than the wild species and grows to half the height, making it ideal amongst low-growing annuals or herbaceous flowers. The foxglove is a modern hybrid. However, the cupid's dart was popular in the seventeenth century, as was the wild *Digitalis purpurea* and its stranger relatives, *D. grandiflora* (greenish yellow) and *D. ferruginea* (rusty brown). A planting of those would be perfect around an old cottage.

This makes a good long-season combination for part of a cottage border, as both plants flower for several months (the foxglove's foliage is good too), and is a perfect filler for a small rose garden.

The genus *Digitalis* is increasingly fashionable and has some attractive species: *D. grandiflora* has forms with different tan-yellow flowers; *D. ferruginea*, tight spires of reddish brown. A newish hybrid, with narrow rose-flushed trumpets, is 'Glory of Roundway'. However, none have exactly the colour of *D.* x *mertonensis*. Catananche also comes in white, and white and blue, though neither has the impact of the ordinary blue type.

cultivation The foxglove is easy from seed, though will only start flowering in its second season, but unlike the wild *Digitalis purpurea*, it will live for a couple of seasons thereafter. That said, old plants do look scrappy, so you are still better off sowing seed every season. Cupid's dart is a vigorous perennial, easily grown from seed; plants are also readily available in garden centres. Once established, it will seed itself mildly, saving you any further expense. Both foxgloves and cupid's dart like sun or light shade, and good rich soil.

extending the grouping In the example shown, there are trails of the soft pink rose scrambling through, but the combination's colours suit almost any of the old roses, and many modern cultivars, too. Green-flowered plants would add contrast, perhaps bells of Ireland (*Molucella laevis*) amongst the foxgloves, and *Alchemilla mollis* or clumps of mignonette in front of the cupid's dart.

previous page left
Helen Dillon's own garden demonstrates her imaginative use of mauves, blues and silver with touches of cerise and yellow.
right *Eryngium alpinum*, an easy and tough perennial, has good flower heads for a month or two.
left Piet Oudolf combines *Monarda* 'Fishes' with *Salvia* x *superba*, topped with a *Phlox* 'Blue Paradise' in a border at Green Farm Plants.
far left The foxglove does not need staking, though the cupid's dart may need it if you prefer a tidy garden.

bergamot and salvia

Bergamots (*Monarda*) are underused in most gardens, which is a shame as they range in colour from white to deepest mauve, are self-supporting and have a long flowering season. The subtlety of their colours and the form of the flower heads allow some elegant combinations in the border, including their pairing with salvias, a grouping most popular amongst modern designers.

This rather dreamy late-summer planting looks lovely bordering a lawn, with the border itself overhung by old orchard trees, and fronted with a trim box hedge. It would make a good margin to a vegetable garden, especially one using the plants on page 76–7. A hotter scheme than the one shown can be created with *Monarda* 'Croftway Pink', either the salvia used here or *Salvia nemerosa*, and – right over the top – a cerise phlox. Alternatively one of the attractive silvery-lilac (*Phlox maculata* 'Alpha') or even white phloxes would be just as effective – *P. paniculata* 'Alba Grandiflora' has the added bonus of a marvellous scent.

cultivation Both plants are vigorous perennials which need little attention. Both are clump forming and can become very crowded; you will probably find you need to divide them every two or three seasons. The bergamot can be propagated from the tiniest pieces. Rich, moist soil and sun or light shade suit both species.

extending the grouping Monardas get a bit leafless on their lower stems, so the combination could usefully have something to cover bare shanks. Catmints like *Nepeta* 'Six Hills Giant' and especially *N. sibirica* 'Souvenir d'André Chaudron' would fit the bill.

Margery Fish

right Mrs Fish liked 'silvers' – from plants like *Stachys byzantina*, and *Santolina chamaecyparissus*, to artemisias, anthemis species and *Convolvulus cneorum*. Extra interest is given by adding jagged green foliage plants and touches of colour.

far right below A collection of cottage plants including *Euphorbia characias*, a favourite species, evergreen *Chamaecyparis lawsoniana* 'Fletcheri',

MARGERY FISH FIRST BECAME INTERESTED IN GARDENS AND GARDEN plants when she and her husband bought East Lambrook Manor in Somerset in 1938. A pleasant and unpretentious house with a couple of acres of ground, it was more or less derelict when they arrived. By her death, in 1969, the garden had become one of the most influential in the country.

Though she got to know neighbouring 'grand' gardens, and went on collecting trips with their owners, she became fascinated by the tiny gardens of her own village and those nearby, especially by some of the old-fashioned plants they still contained.

She popularized these plants in her delightfully readable books: *Cottage Garden Flowers* (1961) is especially good. In her own garden, she put plants together in ways familiar to the villagers, mixing wild valerian with flowering culinary sage *(Salvia officinalis)* and a trailing campanula, or hellebores and gladdon *(Iris foetidissima)*.

She also advocated 'jungle' planting, so that weeds were suppressed, but found that some of her most precious plants, such as *Astrantia major ssp. involucrata* 'Shaggy' were almost as aggressive as weeds. She and her husband did all their garden work themselves, and so labour-intensive drifts of flowers in the Jekyll manner, or even in the style of Sissinghurst Castle (Mrs Fish greatly admired Vita Sackville-West) were not possible. Though she designed no other gardens, her own garden was much visited. Everyone was entranced by her ability to make small-scale plant combinations 'sing', and as she had opened a small nursery, they could also buy the plants for themselves. The garden at East Lambrook Manor is still much as she left it, and can still be visited by the public.

above Self-sown aquilegias contrast with the young leaves of *Rheum palmatum*, which will grow and add to the look of this 'jungle' planting.

Plantsmen's Borders

above Plantsmens' plants aren't necessarily more difficult to grow than the ones found at every garden centre. Here, unusual varieties make sumptuous drifts of colour.

centre A planting featuring the unusual bistort *Persicaria amplexicaule* 'Firetail', a member of a genus with many interesting and seldom-grown forms including pink and orange ones. Behind it is a variety of *Echinops bannaticus*, 'Taplow Blue', which has very large heads of flowers, and is part of another genus with much to explore.

THERE HAVE BEEN PLANT COLLECTORS SINCE TIME immemorial. Even ancient Babylonian kings made long lists of their plants; one such list, dating from around 1000BC, catalogued the vegetables, fruit and medicinal herbs in the royal gardens. Further east, some Chinese paeony records date from 700AD and chrysanthemum lists exist from the same period. Even then, plant collectors must have scanned them enviously, determined to have every species listed.

In Europe, the first garden inventories, like Sir Thomas Hanmer's *Garden Book* (1659) and John Rea's *Flora* (1665) appeared in the seventeenth century. They became so popular that quite large numbers survive, and the competitive element in plantsmens' gardening was well and truly established.

North American plants were collected in the early seventeenth century, but they were mostly grown by European gardeners; it is not clear if American gardeners were as greedy for their native flora, for even by the 1840s, when the landscape gardener Andrew Jackson Downing suggested a list of plants for borders, he included many old-fashioned European plants, but only a few native Americans.

It is hard to say whether the lack of documentation about planting schemes before 1800 means that no one felt that they merited recording, or that the conventions observed were so universal there seemed no need to put them down on paper.

A plantsman collects and uses in his or her plantings rare, new, obscure or sophisticated plants. Connoisseurs admire *Papaver orientale* 'Sultana' (strawberry-pink) or 'Cedric Morris' (palest lavender-grey) rather than the scarlet species; they prefer *Lysimachia atropurpurea* with its strange purple spikes to the ordinary yellow *L. punctata*. Plantsmens' plants are not 'better' or more difficult to grow, but they do allow subtler or more painterly effects than their more widely grown relatives.

The present day is the great age of plantsman designers. Never before has there been such widespread interest in plants and plantings, or so much imagination brought to bear on the garden's flora. Designer gardens have become places of pilgrimage and great designers famous, even cult, figures.

anemones and chrysanthemums

In the 1860s, a Scotswoman called Miss Frances Hope, a noted garden writer of the day, described a grand mixed bed containing white Japanese anemones (*Anemone* x *hybrida*) and deep red chrysanthemums (*Dendranthema*). The cool pinkish white of the anemones and the architecture of their buds and fallen flowers was richly juxtaposed with the deep foliage and multi-petalled flowers of the chrysanthemum. The planting was originally intended as a filling for a large bed, which Miss Hope suggested edging with a brown-leaved heuchera; it would do equally well for a late-summer border.

Miss Hope used the stately *Anemone* x *hybrida* 'Honorine Jobert', new in 1858. She also would have used one of the new Chinese chrysanthemums: today 'Yvonne Arnaud' or 'George Griffiths' would be ideal. Or reverse the colours and plant *A.* x *hybrida* 'Bressingham Glow', in deep rose-purple, amongst white chrysanthemums.

cultivation Both plants are easy perennials, though in cold gardens it is wise to lift the chrysanthemum and overwinter it under cover. That way you can take cuttings of the young shoots that sprout from the root in spring. The plants will do best in sun or light shade, and good soil, but be warned – the anemone can be invasive.

extending the grouping Incorporate a touch of silver – either cardoons (see page 74) or an artemisia like 'Silver Queen'.

anemones and asters

A late-summer classic often used by Gertrude Jekyll, though this planting uses modern hybrids like *Anemone* x *hybrida* 'Bressingham Glow' with tones of *Aster novae-angliae* 'Lye End Beauty', a hybrid that appeared in an English garden in 1958. Though the New England asters have been in Europe since 1710, this is one of the best, its pink only surpassed by 'Andenkenan Alma Pötschke', but that cultivar is too short to plant with the anemones in this combination.

Anemones come in some attractive doubles: equally pink is 'Margarete'; 'Lady Gilmour' is paler. It is also worth planting the species that have given rise to the hybrids, like *A. hupehensis*, with petals in two shades of pink and unequal sizes. Other good New Englander asters include pure white 'Herbstschnee'.

cultivation Both plants are tough, creeping perennials, happy in almost every part of the garden, though the anemones do not like dense shade. Both tolerate drought and poor soil.

extending the grouping If you find this level of colour saturation overpowering, add some plants to cool it down. Either include more *Aster* species, like the charming tiny white *A. divaricatus* or *A. turbinellus* in pinky violet, or add 'silvers' like *Artemisia ludoviciana* 'Silver Queen' or the feathery *A.* 'Powis Castle'.

far left The anemone used in this combination is *A.* 'Königin Charlotte' of 1898. Chrysanthemum varieties come and go quickly, but look for forms of *Dendranthema* Rubellum group. Many are Victorian, and some, like the pink-mauve 'Emperor of China', are ancient orientals.

above As summer wanes, there is less to do in the garden, so put late-flowering perennials like these anemones and asters next to a seat, where they can be easily enjoyed.

gladiolus and
cistus

A ravishing haze of colour from Beth Chatto's garden in Essex, in which several basic combinations can be seen, though the blinding cerise-red of gladiolus and the soft pinks of the cistus (try the hardy 'Silver Pink'), are the key which hold the mix together. The other pinks from thalictrums, soft yellows and greys add harmonies and enough yellow discord to keep things exciting.

There are a number of similar *Gladiolus* species, which are available in varying shades of magenta and are mostly smaller. If you want to try pink or white, explore some of the enchanting Nanus hybrids, though, being part African, they are less hardy. Cistuses have flowers from purest white to sharp pinks and reds, some attractively spotted at the centre. Some species have splendidly aromatic foliage.

The basic combination suits almost any sunny garden, but it is a particularly good cottage planting, while the whole assemblage would make a substantial herbaceous planting for a grander country garden.

cultivation The European gladiolus is a tough, sometimes invasive, bulb, easily grown from seed – indeed, it seeds itself once you have it. Unlike its larger African relatives, it is hardy in most gardens. Some *Cistus* species are not hardy; check that a planned purchase is hardy in your area. All make open shrubs, leggy in age, but easily renewed by cuttings. *C.* 'Elma' has aromatic foliage and huge white flowers that last but a day. Both species like full sun and poorish, dryish soil.

extending the grouping The foreground largely consists of *Euphorbia* x *martinii*. Further back there are clumps of *Verbascum chaixii*, *Erysimum* 'Bowles' Mauve' and *Artemisia* 'Powis Castle'. Dotted amongst the gladioli are alliums and pink *Thalictrum aquilegiifolium*.

rock roses and poppies

Orange is often ignored in the average garden; but it certainly isn't in this planting created by Nori and Sandra Pope at Hadspen House in Somerset. A pale orange form of *Papaver orientale* is set dramatically against a loud orange rock rose (*Helianthemum* 'Henfield Brilliant') – the one floppy and languid, the other very noisy indeed. Within a season or so, they'll be gently harmonized by the bronze fennel planted between them.

Helianthemums come in a number of brilliant yellows, oranges, buffs and pinks. As the poppy can be greyish white, pale amethyst, strawberry-pink, bruise-purple and the usual scarlet, some exciting colour combinations are possible. I would like buff helianthemums with the grey-violet poppy 'Cedric Morris', or the strawberry-pink poppy 'Turkish Delight' with a shocking-pink helianthemum.

This makes a good planting for a front garden, and its mix of loose and tight textures suits a suburban site.

cultivation The poppy is an easy and reliable perennial; the helianthemum a tough little shrub. Both like sun and can cope with poor, dryish soil. Grand forms of this poppy need to be propagated by root cuttings: excavate the soil away on one third of the root area (late autumn is ideal) and expose a few of the broad fleshy roots. Remove as many as you need, slice into 5–8cm (2–3in) lengths, and bury horizontally in a pot. Keep cool, moist and shaded.

extending the grouping *Rosa glauca* or *R. moyesii* will give height to the planting, the former having reddish stems up to 2.5m (8ft) high, blue-green foliage and a brief season of small pink flowers (followed by orange hips). The bush *Rosa moyesii* is equally tall with even showier hips while *Papaver atlanticum*, whose double and single forms flower well into late autumn, will extend the duration of the orange colour scheme. Brightly coloured *Asclepias tuberosa* can be added in a warm garden; *Alstroemeria aurantiaca* will do as well in cooler climates. Orange day lilies (*Hemerocallis* species) were also used in the planting shown above.

eremurus and poppies

The English plantswoman Beth Chatto is renowned for putting interesting plants together in unusual ways. The basic colour scheme of this luxurious planting is laid down by the huge yellow spires of the eremurus and the simple purple flowers of the annual *Papaver somniferum*. The eremerus here is probably a selection from one of the hybrid strains. Try also *Eremurus himalaicus* in purest white (further interest is provided when its seed pods form), and *E. robustus*, which is bigger and shell-pink.

This planting is especially good in formal gardens, around a small square lawn with a central square pool.

cultivation Both species like sun and will do well in dryish soils. Eremurus are easily grown perennials in all but the coldest gardens. The poppy is an annual; for more details see page 137.

extending the grouping Height and bulk are given here by small trees. Tamarisk (*Tamarix* species), with its smoky-purplish flowers, would look good, as would the wild olive (*Elaeagnus angustifolia*).

canna and verbena

First grown in Europe in the 1600s, canna lilies featured in every subtropical bedding scheme 200 years later. This planting by Christopher Lloyd in his garden at Great Dixter (see page 104) is of a canna, probably 'Wyoming', whose burgundy-flushed leaves contrast with the purple pom-poms of *Verbena bonariensis* held high on their wiry stems. Subtropical gardens can use this planting for a whole scheme; in cooler ones, it makes a dramatic filler for a prominently placed bed or a large container.

cultivation Both plants need warm gardens and rich soil, and will overwinter only in mild conditions. In a cold garden, you will have to lift the cannas in winter: if your garden is cold and windy, it is probably not worth trying them at all. The verbena will stand some frost, so it is simpler to treat it as an annual or to overwinter plants under glass.

extending the grouping In turn-of-the-century gardens, verbena was often partnered by pelargoniums, so add a deep red or violet-red flowered one such as 'Lord Bute', a regal group pelargonium.

right Eremurus and poppy are set off by *Verbascum bombyciferum*, alliums and some bearded irises.

far right above In warm climates, plantings of canna and pachystachys are often used for showy beds in the lawn.

far right below A dramatic planting of canna and verbena is suitable for a mild corner of the garden or a conservatory.

canna and
pachystachys

This planting from Longwood Garden in Pennsylvania suits a warm, shaded spot or a conservatory and looks good by a pool or fountain, or by a cluster of large pots. The yellow- and green-striped leaves of the canna are echoed in the yellow bracts and green leaves of the fast-growing *Pachystachys lutea*. The planting will be even more interesting when the canna flowers.

cultivation Both plants are from tropical America, so need warmth, moisture and good feeding. Watch out for slug damage, and for red spider mite if you are growing them under glass, and if not, give the canna some protection as its foliage can be damaged without shelter. Pachystachys soon makes a small bush, but as older plants can become leggy it is best propagated by spring cuttings each year. The canna forms clumps which are easily divided at the season's end.

extending the grouping Start with a bamboo such as *Phyllostachys nigra* and wrap the canna planting round it. Underplant the combination with a fern like *Adiantum cretica* 'Albolineata'.

far right So many gardeners plant only for flowers, yet planting for seed heads or dead stems can create some striking combinations. This planting of ipomoea and fennel is best in the autumn.

right Sedges and their relatives have some extraordinary foliage colours that offer opportunities for imaginative groupings such as its pairing with euphorbia, as shown here.

euphorbia and
sedge

Euphorbias and sedges are made for one another. This pairing of bronze-leaved sedge (*Carex buchananii*), a recent introduction from New Zealand, and the sometimes reddish-leaved *Euphorbia* x *martinii* is a striking example. By teaming *Carex elata* 'Aurea' (formerly known as *C. stricta* 'Bowles' Golden') with a yellow or bronze *Euphorbia polychroma* cultivar, you can create a yellow–based scheme. Or go

bigger, with a large sedge like *Carex pendula* and *Euphorbia characias*, for a perfect shade planting in an urban garden.

The combination could either be used in a sophisticated modern bedding scheme, with squares of sedge outlined with the euphorbia, for example, and the whole set in a paved yard; or it could be an informal planting in a wildish part of the garden.

cultivation The euphorbia makes a low spreading bush and is hardy in all but the coldest gardens. It can be propagated by taking cuttings of young shoots. The sedge is an evergreen perennial, eventually making dense clumps, which can be divided in early spring. Both plants prefer shade and moist soil, but will tolerate sun and drought.

extending the grouping The pairing works well with any of the fern and hosta combinations shown on pages 52–5. The colour scheme can be accentuated in spring by adding some bronze-red tulips or a soft yellow species like *Tulipa sylvestris*, which also has the advantage of being perfumed.

ipomoea and fennel

This witty late-summer planting at the Botanic Gardens in Washington D.C. combines fennel (*Foeniculum vulgare*) with the entwining dark purple form of *Ipomoea hederacea*, whose bells contrast superbly with the dying flowerstalks of the herb.

There are a number of climbing ipomoeas. The lovely 'morning glory' in sky blue is now called *Ipomoea tricolor* 'Heavenly Blue' but there is no need to worry about the name – just grow it. Instead of fennel, why not grow the climber up through angelica (*Angelica archangelica*), or even amongst rhubarb that has been allowed to flower and seed?

A corner of the kitchen or cottage garden can be home to this planting, next to an arch covered with a mid-pink rose. Or you could include it as a vertical accent in a bed of butternut squashes.

cultivation Fennel is a tough perennial that improves season by season, but the ipomoea is best treated as an annual. Ipomoeas won't grow well outdoors in cool summer gardens, but if your garden has a sheltered spot, start seed off indoors in late winter or early spring, and plant the seedlings out when the last frost has gone. Examine the young plants regularly while they are still under glass as they can be prone to greenfly. In frost-free gardens, you can sow seed outdoors once spring arrives.

extending the grouping Plant this combination by a bower or pergola and add late-flowering clematis and roses (see the combinations on pages 24–7 for ideas).

aster and euphorbia

Many gardeners grow large-flowered asters, yet amongst the species with tiny flowers there are some true delights to be discovered. Here a hybrid called *Aster* 'Combe Fishacre', with drifts of tiny pink flowers with ruby centres, is deftly paired with the blue-green leaves of the shrubby *Euphorbia characias wulfenii*, for a grand late-summer planting. Few other asters have quite this degree of charm, though *Aster turbinellus* is almost as good. Most of the species grow in light scrub; in the garden they can need staking. If using a single cane for each plant, take care that they do not look like a sheaf of corn.

Dozens of lovely asters are available, such as *A. ericoides* 'Hon Vicary Gibbs' or *A. novae-angliae* 'Lye End Beauty' if you want something larger. Even violet Michaelmas daisies look splendid with the euphorbia, for which there is no real substitute.

It is a sophisticated colour scheme, so try it beside a grand seat that catches the evening sun in late summer: you'll probably want a few pots of lilies and some deep violet heliotropes close by to heighten the effect.

cultivation The aster is a tough perennial needing division every few seasons, but little other care. The euphorbia makes a bush up to 1.2–1.5m (4–5ft) across and similarly high. In cold gardens it really needs the protection of a wall; in milder conditions, it can still be short lived, but at least there are usually some self-sown seedlings nearby to replace dying plants. Flower spikes begin to form in early spring and can be large when fully expanded. Brilliant yellow-green or slightly brownish, it is a plant with a long season of interest.

Both species like sun or partial shade, and can put up with poor soil, but be warned that neither likes damp.

extending the grouping I have a planting like this that also includes artichokes, *Penstemon* 'Burgundy' and clumps of *Crocosmia masoniorum*. Alternatively, the grass *Helictotrichon sempervirens* makes a useful contribution to the basic combination and an artemisia like *A. ludoviciana* 'Silver Queen' would be good. A combination of brunnera and pulmonaria can be used to fill out the foreground.

left To create this colour scheme earlier in the season, follow the example of Margery Fish and plant valerian (*Centranthus ruber*) throughout the combination. The euphorbia is ideal with pink old roses like 'Comte de Chambord' or 'Chapeau de Napoléon'. Neither the aster nor the euphorbia is perfumed; in gardens with very little frost, try *Euphorbia mellifera*, which has good foliage and dramatic flower spikes that smell sweetly of honey.

right A good way to soften brilliant scarlet or cerise is to add softer tones of the same colour, and a touch of something sharper still. Here, some fine plantsmen's plants have been added to the pairing.
far right The strange *Paris polyphylla*, with its extraordinary flower heads, stands out amongst a drift of *Astrantia major*. This form of astrantia has pinkish fertile florets and is a popular choice for a plantsman's garden.

indigofera and flax

This startling planting, from Folkington Place in East Sussex, teams an unusual shrub, *Indigofera heterantha*, which has been recorded in gardens since the sixteenth century though is rarely grown today, with the cerise-flowered annual flax (*Linum grandiflorum* 'Rubrum'). The soft and subtle shades of the indigofera make it a perfect foil.

There are few species of indigofera and this is definitely the best for most gardens. Though there are many varieties of linum, this is the nicest red, but it is still worthwhile experimenting with the rich blue *Linum perenne* 'Blau Saphir'. The indigofera is, as its name suggests, the plant that yields the violet-blue dye indigo, or 'anil'. Its production was mostly carried out in American plantations, and the dye used locally or exported to Europe. The linum is a close relative of the commercial flax plant (*Linum usitatissimum*), which is a tall, blue-flowered annual.

Site the combination against a sunny wall or fence, in a garden of almost any style. To keep the planting in order, tie some of the indigofera's branches into the wall; you could even use it to shade the roots of a clematis.

cultivation Indigoferas make low, spreading, deciduous bushes, which need a sunny wall or winter protection in cold gardens. As they are not always long lived, it is as well to save seed or take cuttings in late spring. The annual flax can be sown in the open ground once the soil has warmed up in late spring.

extending the grouping Stands of the delightful *Geranium wallichianum* 'Buxton's Variety' feature in this planting; a species with more dominant foliage, such as *Geranium phaeum* 'Samobor', with spots and bands of deep brown-purple, would look even better. Sphaeralcea would also be a good addition; the subtle tones of its flowers provide a foil for the brighter ones of the indigofera. Try the sprawling *Sphaeralcea munroana*. Finish off by creating a backdrop of some of the rose and clematis pairs on pages 24–7.

paris and astrantia

The very rare *Paris polyphylla*, a Himalayan relative of the smaller and more familiar European herb Paris (*Paris quadrifolia*), makes an unusual counterpart to a drift of old-fashioned *Astrantia major* (Hattie's pincushion). Its emphatic foliage and strange brown flower spikes offset the astrantia's greenish-ivory and pink flower heads and haze of foliage.

The Paris is almost unique; of the other species, *P. japonica* is similar but even rarer still. *P. quadrifolia*, a European native, is only 15cm (6in) high, but as an alternative to something as unusual as *P. polyphylla*, use *Podophyllum peltatum*, similar in form, whose young leaves are dappled in purple. Podophyllums (or 'May apple') have white or palest pink flowers, followed by pendant fruits.

The best of the greenish-white astrantias is in my opinion, *A. major* ssp. *involucrata* 'Shaggy', though there are also deep mahogany-red forms like 'Hadspen Blood'. If you plan to use podophyllums, try some of the dusky-pink forms of *Astrantia maxima*.

None of the podophyllums are common in garden centres, but they are easily raised from seed. All like shade, moisture and rich soil. They set seed easily, and will even self-seed.

Shady woodland margins or clearings are the most natural place for this planting, especially with a pool nearby. Buildings create plenty of shade too, of course, making it suitable for urban gardens.

cultivation The Paris is a long-lasting perennial, slowly increasing. If you buy specimens from different sources, your plants may cross-pollinate and you may be lucky enough to get big orange seed pods, and hence many seedlings. The astrantia is a tough perennial and is easily propagated by division. Both species like part or full shade along with dampish soil.

extending the grouping Other shade lovers will mix in happily – astilbes and osmundas or solomon's seal and hellebores (see the combination on page 57). The combination could also be enhanced by adding *Rodgersia* 'Parasol' along with sheaves of white *Veronicastrum virginicum*, as well as the form of *Geranium phaeum* which has plummy-black flowers.

sedums and
grasses

The larger sedums, with their broad waxen leaves and flat heads of flowers in late summer, have a natural affinity with grasses. The pinks and rusty rose-reds of the sedum flowers complement the tawny greens and silvers of the arching grass stems.

Grasses suitable for use in this combination include *Calamagrostis* x *acutiflora* and the glittering purple-headed *Melica altissima* 'Atropurpurea'. Blue-leaved grasses can work well too, particularly with sedums with very glaucous foliage; try *Helictotrichon sempervirens* for a grass to go amongst sedums, or *Stipa gigantea* to arch above them. Grass flower spikes contrast well with sedums; try adding the delightful *Hordeum jubatum*.

Sedums which work well are *S. spectabile* or *S. telephium*, and their cultivars, including *S. spectabile* 'Brilliant' in a softer pink and 'Septemberglut'. Don't bother with the white ones.

This combination can be treated in the modern manner, as big overlapping drifts in part of a contemporary garden. More traditionally, it could form the basis of a red border, to be joined by penstemons, dahlias, clumps of kniphofia and so on.

cultivation Both species are sound perennials, but the grass can sometimes be a nuisance if you let its runners take hold. Be ruthless and yank out stems that spread too far, otherwise the sedum will rapidly die out if it gets swamped. Most grasses run, or can easily be propagated by division. *Sedum spectabile* and its allies can be divided in spring; simply pull the shoots apart. Many of them will already have rootlets at their base; if not, they are easily treated as cuttings. Both plants prefer sun and good soil, but are not averse to partial shade or even poor soil.

extending the grouping As in the planting shown left, you could introduce *Polygonum amplexicaule*. Or add almost any kniphofia (as shown top right), from the yellow 'Little Maid' or 'Percy's Pride' to huge salmon-rose varieties like 'John Benary'. To keep the purplish-red theme going, simply add a dark red form of *Astrantia major* for a really thunderous colouring.

far left The richly coloured *Sedum* 'Herbstfreude' smoulders against the chilly elegance of *Phalaris arundinacea* var. *picta* 'Feesey'. The grass has been cut back hard earlier in the summer.

above Verticals and horizontals make a striking combination. Not all kniphofias flower in late summer; check your variety first. The red-and-yellow *Kniphofia uvaria* is recommended, but try 'Royal Standard' too. 'Brimstone' is a good late yellow that is worth trying.

left An extraordinary planting, combining a purple-leaved hybrid of *Sedum telephium* (possibly 'Vera Jameson') with a deep red *Astrantia major*. It is cooled by a pale achillea, but silver artemisias, especially *A. ludoviciana* 'Powis Castle', could also be used.

right Light woodland suits this planting of corydalis and ferns though it can adapt to urban shade. I have something similar in the shade of pots next to a tiny watertank.

below Solidago and silphium make an ideal prairie planting, perhaps around a shack for catching the last of summer.

solidago and
silphium

The Dutch artist and gardener Ton ter Linden is responsible for this tapestry of yellows, greens and grey-blues using *Silphium terebinthaceum* and golden rod (*Solidago*). Silphium, introduced from America in the eighteenth century, has vast blue-green leaves that offset its own cold yellow flowers and the warmer yellow sprays of golden rod. The pairing comes into its own in late summer, when many other plantings are fading.

Golden rods do not have a vast range, but you can find denser forms, and some with paler or more ochre-yellows. There are other silphium species, including *S. laciniatum*, with dramatically cut leaves.

cultivation Silphium and golden rod are tough, hardy perennials, liking sun and rich, moist soil, though they tolerate less favourable conditions. They can be invasive, so restrain them where necessary and, to keep them at their best, divide clumps every few seasons.

extending the grouping Add, as here, rudbeckias. Or try some of the bigger grasses, like *Miscanthus sinensis*, or even pampas grass, and early asters in blue – look out for cultivars of *Aster novi-belgii*.

corydalis and ferns

Athyrium niponicum var. *pictum* is one of the most exotic small ferns, with low purplish foliage; each leaflet is sometimes almost silvery towards its centre. In a detail from a planting by the American-based designer Wolfgang Oehme, it looks enchanting with the wild *Corydalis lutea*, the two sorts of foliage making a good counterpoint, sharpened by the clusters of yellow corydalis flowers.

There are a number of easy corydalis species to try. Another yellow species is the handsome *C. cheilanthifolia*, with long, frilled leaves, which are brownish green when young. Try, too, some of the vigorous forms of *C. flexuosa*, which have large flowers in shades of blue.

cultivation The fern and the corydalis like cool, damp, shaded conditions, and will do well on suitable walls, paving or even in a container. Both plants are hardy, the corydalis being a tough perennial. Snails like to graze the young fronds of the fern and can do the plant mortal damage, so keep watch as the leaves first unfurl.

extending the grouping A carpet of even smaller greenery will make a distinctive background: try *Soleirolia soleirolii* (if you dare), *Mentha requienii* or even *Lysimachia nummularia*.

artemisia and verbascum

Artemisia ludoviciana 'Silver Queen' is a fine plant to have in any garden, but teamed here by Ton ter Linden with *Verbascum blattaria* f. *albiflorum* it makes a stunning combination. The silver of the artemisia and the off-white verbascum flowers are a perfect foil for the sharp pinks and mauves of the other plants.

There are plenty of silver artemisias, but this cultivar was chosen because of its strongly vertical growth. The ordinary *Verbascum blattaria* has brownish-violet flowers, but there are many others, like the beautiful *V. chaixii* 'Cotswold Queen' with honey-coloured flowers.

cultivation Both artemisias and verbascums are perennials. The artemisia runs vigorously, so thin it out regularly to keep it within bounds. The verbascum is weakly perennial, so treat it as a biennial and harvest and sow seed each year. Both like sun and good soil.

extending the grouping The example shown here includes *Campanula lactiflora*, which can be complemented by companion clumps of soft pink *C. lactiflora* 'Loddon Anna'. Put some deep violet-black hollyhocks at the back and set thug against thug by introducing forms of *Campanula punctata* amongst the artemisias.

left The combination of artemisia and verbascum is crisp enough to work in an urban site or in a cottage border. An ivy-covered wall makes an ideal backdrop. The violet-spiked plant at the back is *Veronicastrum virginianum* 'Fascination', which was discovered by Ton ter Linden.

eryngium and
artemisia

In a combination that will thrive in a dry, gravelly garden, the wiry silver foliage of *Artemisia alba* 'Canescens' contrasts with the broad and ferociously spiny bracts of *Eryngium giganteum* 'Silver Ghost'. Piet Oudolf devised this fine contemporary planting for the gardens of Green Farm Plants in Hampshire.

This is the only eryngium that has ruffs which look as if they should be adorning a dinosaur, and which last so long in the season. There are lots of good artemisias: the shrubby and creeping *A. pontica is* worth planting, while you could add broad-leaved *A. stelleriana* for a touch of pure white. Some helichrysums are ideal, though the familiar curry plant (*Helichrysum angustifolium*), smells too strongly of its namesake to make a good garden plant, especially if planted near a seat.

A dry sun-baked border is a good spot for this combination, though the eryngium will still grow happily in lusher conditions. A sunny and rocky slope would be ideal, especially if it has steps that the artemisia can sprawl over.

cultivation The artemisia is a low sprawling shrub. The eryngium is biennial, though once you have plants, if you leave the flower heads to ripen, you will soon have a succession of seedlings

extending the grouping The planting shown includes *Santolina pinnata* ssp. *neapolitana* 'Edward Bowles', with silver foliage and cream-mustard flowers. The santolina flowers have a pungent aroma, and some gardeners keep the bushes clipped to stop them flowering; it is worth doing this every second season or two to keep the bushes compact, ensuring they don't split apart when you do let them flower. You could also try *Verbascum* 'Frosted Gold', but the combination would benefit from some deep blues too, perhaps from the most thrilling of all the salvias, *Salvia patens* (you will have to lift the tubers in cold gardens), though *S. farinacea* is good, too. Lavenders are also recommended: 'Giant White' is the tallest, and looks splendid with eryngiums. *Lavandula* x *intermedia* Old English Group is amongst the most fragrant, and responds well to clipping.

left Late-afternoon light makes this planting of eryngium, artemisia and santolina look especially luxurious; bees, especially bumble bees, are attracted to the eryngium flowers and seem to find the nectar a soporific. The artemisia produces short spires of greeny-yellow daisies. It will need cutting back when it gets leggy.

Wolfgang Oehme and James van Sweden

right Tight purple spikes of *Lirope muscari*, from Eastern Asia, sedums and grasses are planted in broad swathes of soft colour, almost a northern equivalent of some of the tropical plantings created by Roberto Burle Marx.
far right below The Oehme/van Sweden style is shown to great effect with gold *Calamagrostis acutiflora* 'Karl Foerster' mixed with *Echinacea purpurea*, the blue-purple of *Perovskia atriplicifolia*, yellow *Rudbeckia fulgida* 'Goldsturm' and purple *Monarda* 'Purpurkrone'.

WOLFGANG OEHME AND JAMES VAN SWEDEN BRING A SPECIAL FEELING FOR plants to their busy landscape and garden design practice based in Washington D.C. Their commissions span most of the US, and cross the Atlantic to the Netherlands and Germany. Oehme earned his credentials as a horticulturist and landscape architect in his native Germany, and came to practise in the United States in 1957. James van Sweden has studied and worked in urban design, both in the Netherlands and the United States.

Exuberant, informal sweeps of herbaceous perennials and decorative grasses characterize their often quite formal designs, where any built elements are incorporated to anchor the garden firmly to the ground plan.

With a wide, and still increasing, knowledge of plants of all sorts, their use of them to make exciting combinations is becoming widely influential. Teaming skimmias with *Mahonia japonica* and *Nandina domestica*, they created a shade and shrub-layer planting, perfect for small urban spaces. Though some of the species used are non-American, Oehme and van Sweden's work over the past decade or so is increasingly devoted to the American flora, using trees and shrubs like *Magnolia virginiana*, sourwood (*Oxydendrum arboreum*) and serviceberry (*Amelanchier* species), as well as many herbaceous species from the prairies.

Their 'New American Garden' style is a metaphor, they say, for the American meadow and its astoundingly rich mix of species. However, they acknowledge that prairies are not typical of the entire US and also produce clever and beautiful shrub and tree plantings that emulate the complex layered structure of natural woodland.

above A late-summer detail of *Pennisetum alopecuroides* 'Moudry', and purple *Aster tataricus* along with several pretty white flowers of *Anemone hybrida* 'Honorine Jobert'.

gardens to visit

UNITED KINGDOM

Barnsley House Garden
Barnsley, nr Cirencester, Gloucestershire
Open Mon, Wed, Thur, Sat; 10am–6pm or dusk
Rosemary Verey's brilliant planning and plantings.

East Lambrook Manor
East Lambrook, near South Petherton, Somerset
Open Mar–Oct daily except Sunday; 10am–5pm
Margery Fish's cottage style garden.

Great Dixter
Northiam, 8m NW of Rye, East Sussex
Open Mar–Oct, daily except Monday; 11am–5pm
Huge variety of plants and topiary garden.

Green Farm Plants
Bury Court, Bentley, nr Farnham, Hampshire
Open all year, Wed–Sat; 10am–6pm
Plantings designed by Piet Oudolf.

Hadspen Garden
2m SE of Castle Cary, Somerset
Open Mar–Sept, Thurs–Sun and bank hol Mon
9am–6pm
*Superb garden housing the National Rodgersia
Collection.*

Hestercombe
Cheddon Fitzpaine, nr Taunton, Somerset
Open daily; 10am–6pm (winter closes at 5pm)
Beautifully restored and a Jekyll masterpiece.

Hidcote Manor
Hidcote Bartrim, nr Chipping Campden,
Gloucestershire
Open Apr–Sept, daily except Tues and Fri; 1–7pm
Open Oct, daily except Tues and Fri; 11am–6pm
Lovely combinations by Lawrence Johnston.

Inverewe
Poolewe, Ross and Cromarty, Highland Region
Open Mar–Oct, daily; 9.30am–9.00pm
Rocky peninsula set with rare plants.

Sissinghurst Castle
Sissinghurst, nr Cranbrook, Kent
Open Apr–15th Oct, Tues–Fri; 1pm–6.30pm
(weekends 10am–5.30pm)
Vita Sackville-West's beautiful garden.

Sticky Wicket
Buckland Newton, nr Dorchester, Dorset
Open mid-June–mid-Sept, Thurs only
10.30am–8pm
Colour harmonies carried out with great panache.

West Dean Gardens
5m N of Chichester, Sussex
Open Mar–Oct daily; 11am–5pm
*Mixed and herbaceous borders with kitchen garden
and fruit collection.*

White Barns House
Elmstead Market, Colchester, Essex
Open Mar–Oct, daily except Sunday; 9am–5pm
Open Nov–Feb, Mon–Fri; 9am–4pm
Beth Chatto's splendid garden and nursery.

EIRE

Ballymaloe
Shannagary, Midleton, 30km E of Cork
Open Apr–Oct, daily; 9am–6pm
*Formal decorative kitchen garden and stylish
herbaceous borders.*

FRANCE

Giverny
Musée Claude Monet, Giverny, 4km E of Vernon
Apr–Oct, daily except Monday; 10am–6pm
*Claude Monet's garden, famous for waterlilies,
irises, roses and nasturtiums.*

Le Bois des Moutiers
Varengeville-sur-Mer, Brittany, France
Open mid-Mar–mid-Nov, Tue–Fri; 10–2, 2–6pm
Sat–Mon; 2–7pm
Garden originally designed by Gertrude Jekyll.

GERMANY

Hermannshof, Weinheim
Town centre
Open Mar–Oct, Tues–Sun; 10am–7pm
Superb plants and plant combinations.

Westpark, Munich
End of Westendstrasse
Open all year, daily; dawn to dusk
Free entry
*Many themed gardens. Particularly good for
'prairie' plantings of herbaceous species.*

NETHERLANDS

Ton ter Linden's Garden
Achterma 20, Ruinen, Drenthe
Open end April–end September, daily except
Monday; 10am–5pm
Entry fl12.50
Marvellous plant combinations.

U.S.A

U.S. National Arboretum
New York Avenue, Washington D.C
Open daily except Christmas day; 8am–5pm
Oehme and van Sweden's innovative design.

left, top to bottom Hadspen House, Somerset;
West Dean College, Sussex; Ballymaloe Cookery
School Gardens, Co. Cork; Westpark, Germany
right, top to bottom Great Dixter, East Sussex;
Inverewe, Ross and Cromarty, Highland;
Hermannshof, Germany; Sticky Wicket, Dorset

list of suppliers

The plants named in this book are, on the whole, widely available. Suppliers of those plants which are less easily available are listed below. Those quoted here may not be the only growers; where there were two or three choices, I have given the names of firms of which I have some knowledge.

B & T World Seeds
Paguignan
34210 Olonzac
France
Tel: 00 33 46 89 12 96 3
Sunflowers, *Ipomoea hederacea*
Mail order available worldwide

Blackmore & Langdon Ltd
Pensford
Bristol
Avon
Tel: 01275 332300
Delphinium varieties
Mail order available

The Botanic Nursery
Bath Road
Atworth
Nr. Melksham
Wiltshire SN12 8NU
Tel: 01225 706597
Digitalis 'Glory of Roundway'
Some mail order available

Beth Chatto Gardens Ltd
Elmstead Market
Colchester
Essex CO7 7DB
Tel: 01206 822007
White flowered chives, *Centaurea ruthenica*
Mail order available

Chipchase Castle Nursery
Wark, Hexham
Northumberland
Tel: 01434 230083
Violas
Some mail order available

Coombland Gardens Nursery
Coneyhurst
Billingshurst
W. Sussex
RH14 9DY
Tel: 01403 741727
Ipomoea hederacea
Mail order available

Cotswold Garden Flowers
Sands Lane
Badsey
Evesham
Worcestershire
Tel: 01386 833849
Good range of *Canna* varieties,
Kniphofia 'John Benary'
Mail order available

Crug Farm Plants
Griffith's Crossing
Caernarfon
Gwynedd
Wales LL55 1TU
Tel: 01248 670232
Meconopsis

Jack Drake
Inshriach Alpine Nursery
Aviemore, Invernessshire
Scotland PH22 1QS
Tel: 01540 651287
Violas
Mail order available

Fir Tree Farm Nursery
Tresahor
Constantine
Falmouth
Cornwall TR11 5PL
Tel: 01326 340593
Paris polyphylla
Mail order available

Four Seasons
Fornett St Mary
Norwich
Norfolk NR16 1JT
Tel: 01508 488344
Eryngium giganteum 'Silver Ghost'
Mail order only

Green Farm Plants
Bury Court
Bentley, Farnham
Surrey GU10 5LZ
Tel: 01420 23202
Poppies

Hollington Nurseries
Woolton Hill
Newbury
Berkshire RG20 9XT
Tel: 01635 253908
Salvia involucrata
Mail order available

Lakes' Hardy Plants
4 Fearns Building
Penistone
South Yorkshire S36 6BA
Tel: 01226 370574
Digitalis 'Glory of Roundway'
Mail order available

Manor Nursery
Thaxted Road
Wimbish

Saffron Walden
Essex CB10 2UT
Tel: 01799 513481
Paradisa liliastrum

Monksilver Nursery
Oakington Road
Cottenham
Cambridgeshire CB4 4TW
Tel: 01954 251555
Aster novae-angliae 'Lye End Beauty'
Mail order available

Priorswood Clematis
Priorswood
Widbury Hill
Ware
Hertfordshire SG12 7QH
Tel: 01920 461543
Clematis 'Etoile Rose'
Mail order available

Roseholme Nursery
Roseholme Farm
Howsham
Market Rasen
Lincolnshire LN7 6JZ
Tel: 01652 678661
Paradisea liliastrum
Mail order available

Rougham Hall Nurseries
Ipswich Road
Rougham
Bury St. Edmunds
Suffolk IP30 9LZ
Tel: 01359 270577
Delphinium varieties
Mail order available

The Seed Guild
The Coach House
Carnuath
Lanark ML11 8LF
Tel: 01555 841450
Ipomoea hederacea
Mail order only

Suffolk Herbs Ltd
Monks Farm
Coggeshall Road
Kelvedon
Essex CO5 1PG
Tel: 01376 572456
Wide variety of cabbages and alliums including Brussels sprout 'Rubine'
Mail order only

Index

Page numbers in **bold** indicate plant combinations.
Page numbers in *italics* indicate illustrations.

Acknowledgments

1 Saxon Holt (Keeyla Meadows Garden, California, USA); 2 Andrew Lawson ; 3 Juliette Wade /The Garden Picture Library ; 4– 5 Gary Rogers/The Garden Picture Library; 6 above Sothebys, London; 6 below E.T Archive; 7 Egyptian Museum, Cairo/E.T Archive; 8 Museo Nazionale Romano delle Terme, Rome/AKG, London ; 9 below left Musee du Bardo, Tunis/Gilles Mermet/AKG, London; 9 below right Musee de Cluny, Paris/E.T Archive ; 10 Chateau de Maintenon, France/E.T Archive; 11 left British Library, London/Bridgeman Art Library, London/New York; 11 below right Graphic Collection Albertina, Vienna/Erich Lessing/AKG London; 12 above Kunsthistorisches Museum, Vienna/Erich Lessing/AKG, London; 12 below Badminton House/E.T Archive; 13 Hermitage, St. Petersburg/Bridgeman Art Library, London/New York; 14 above Thyssen-Bornemisza Collection, Madrid/AKG, London; 14 below left Christopher Wood Gallery, London/Bridgeman Art Library, London/New York; 14 below right The Mallett Gallery,London/Bridgeman Art Library. London/New York; 16 Hermitage, St Petersburg/Bridgeman Art Library, London/New York; 17 Osterreichische Galerie, Vienna/Bridgeman Art Library, London/New York; 18–19 Roger Foley; 20 above left J C Mayer-G Le Scanff ('Le Baque' (47), France); 20–21 John Miller/The Garden Picture Library (Sissinghurst, Kent); 22 above John Glover; 22 below Mayer/le Scanff/The Garden Picture Library; 24 Howard Rice/The Garden Picture Library (Royal National Rose Society, Herts); 25 Derek Fell; 26 left Derek Fell; 26–27 Jerry Harpur (Designer Arabella Lennox-Boyd, London); 27 right Roger Foley; 28–29 Lamontagne/The Garden Picture Library (Hidcote Manor, Glos); 29 right Lamontagne/The Garden Picture Library; 31 above Andrew Lawson; 31 below Ursel Borstell (Owner Mrs Toos Gerritsen, Netherlands); 32 Juliette Wade/The Garden Picture Library (Shucklets, Oxon); 33 Mayer/Le Scanff/The Garden Picture Library; 34 right Jerry Harpur (Designer Rosemary Verey/Barnsley House, Glos); 34 left Sunniva Harte (Groombridge Place,Kent); 36 Erika Craddock/The Garden Picture Library (Hestercombe Gardens, Somerset); 37 above John Glover/The Garden Picture Library (Munstead Wood, Surrey); 37 below JS Sira/The Garden Picture Library (Folly Farm, Berkshire); 38–39 Ursel Borstell; 40 left John Glover /The Garden Picture Library (Designer Bunny Guinness, Chelsea Flower Show 1995); 40–41 Ron Evans/The Garden Picture Library; 42 John Glover; 43 Brigitte Thomas /The Garden Picture Library (Giverny, France); 44 John Glover/The Garden Picture Library; 45 S & O Mathews (Hightown Farm, Hants); 46 S & O Mathews (Sir Harold Hillier Gardens and Arboretum, Hants); 47 above S & O Mathew (RHS Wisley, Surrey); 47 below S & O Mathews (RHS Wisley, Surrey); 48–49 S & O Mathews (RHS Wisley, Surrey); 50 above Ursel Borstell (Owner Mrs Lidy Kloeg, Netherlands); 50 below Howard Rice/The Garden Picture Library; 51 Howard Rice/The Garden Picture Library; 52–53 above S & O Mathews; 52–53 centre Sunniva Harte (Spinners Nursery, Hants); 52–53 below Steven Wooster/The Garden Picture Library; 54–55 Ursel Borstell (Owner Mrs Laura Dingemans, Netherlands); 56 Marianne Majerus; 57 above Ursel Borstell (Owner Mrs Laura Dingemans, Netherlands); 57 below Andrew Lawson (East Lambrook Manor, Somerset); 58 S & O Mathews (Little Court, Hants); 59 Juliette Wade (Well Cottage, Herefordshire); 60 left JS Sira /The Garden Picture Library (Savill Garden, Surrey); 60–61 centre Jerry Harpur (Inverewe Garden, Ross & Cromarty, Scotland); 61 right Howard Rice (University of Cambridge Botanic Garden); 62 above Howard Rice (University of Cambridge Botanic Garden); 62 below Andrew Lawson; 63 Kim Blaxland/The Garden Picture Library; 64 Andrew Lawson (Giverny, France); 65 above J C Maye Le Scanff (Fondation Claude Monet (27), France); 65 below S & O Mathews (Claude Monet's Garden,Giverny, France); 66–67 S & O Mathews (RHS Wisley, Surrey); 68 left S & O Mathews (North Court, Isle of Wight); 68–69 J C Mayer-G Le Scanff (Designer Eric Ossart, Festival des Jardins de Chaumont s/Loire (41),France); 70 David Cavagnaro; 71 Ursel Borstell (Nursery Coen Jansen, Netherlands); 72–73 Stephen Robson (Seattle Tilth Garden); 74 Ron Evans/The Garden Picture Library (Woodpeckers, Warcs); 75 above Stephen Robson (Hadspen Garden and Nursery, Somerset); 75 below S & O Mathews; 76 above Jacqui Hurst/The Garden Picture Library (Designer Joy Larkcom); 76 below J C Mayer-G Le Scanff (Domaine de Saint-Jean de Beauregard (91), France); 77 Juliette Wade (Rofford Manor, Oxon); 78–79 Stephen Robson (Sticky Wicket, Dorset); 80–81 John Glover (Sticky Wicket, Dorset); 82 John Ferro Sims/The Garden Picture Library; 83 Jerry Pavia; 84 Andrew Lawson (Designer Rosemary Verey, Barnsley House, Glos); 85 above Jerry Harpur (Designer Rosemary Verey, Barnsley House, Glos); 85 below Jerry Harpur (Designer Rosemary Verey, Barnsley House, Glos); 86–87 Ursel Borstell; 88 left J C Mayer-G Le Scanff (Jardin de Talos (09), France); 88–89 J C Mayer-G Le Scanff (Le Jardin de Campagne (95), France); 90 Henk Dijkman/The Garden Picture Library (Ineke Greve Garden, Netherlands); 91 above Michele Lamontagne; 91 below Andrew Lawson (Designer Wendy Lauderdale); 92–93 John Glover; 94 Juliette Wade/The Garden Picture Library; 95 John Glover; 96 Clive Nichols (Designer Julie Toll); 97 Erika Craddock/The Garden Picture Library (Les Bois des Moutiers, France); 98 above Andrew Lawson (Designer Urs Walser, Hermannshof, Germany); 98 below Sunniva Harte /The Garden Picture Library (Folkington Place, East Sussex); 99 Ken Druse; 100 Steven Wooster/The Garden Picture Library (Park Farm, Essex); 101 Jerry Pavia/The Garden Picture Library; 102–103 above Jerry Harpur (Designers Oehme & Van Sweden, Washington DC,USA); 102–103 centre Piet Oudolf (Designer Piet Oudolf); 102–103 below Piet Oudolf (Designer Piet Oudolf); 104 JS Sira/The Garden Picture Library (Great Dixter, East Sussex); 105 above Jerry Harpur (Great Dixter, East Sussex); 105 below Jerry Harpur (Great Dixter, East Sussex); 106–107 Andrew Lawson (Eastgrove Cottage Nurseries, Worcestershire); 108 left Sunniva Harte (Groombridge Place, Kent); 108–109 Steven Wooster; 110 Jerry Pavia (Grivaz, France); 111 Ron Evans/The Garden Picture Library; 112 Juliette Wade; 113 Howard Rice (Clare College, Cambridge); 114 left Howard Rice; 114–115 centre Howard Rice; 115 right John Glover; 116 above S & O Mathews (Little Court,Hants); 116 below Juliette Wade (Little Court, Hants); 117 S & O Mathews (RHS Wisley,Surrey); 118 Andrew Lawson; 119 above Sunniva Harte; 119 below Marijke Heuff/The Garden Picture Library; 120–121 above S & O Mathews (Sir Harold Hillier Gardens and Arboretum, Hants); 120–121 centre John Glover; 120–121 below Howard Rice (University of Cambridge Botanic Garden); 122–123 Howard Rice (University of Cambridge Botanic Garden); 124 John Glover /The Garden Picture Library (Dillon Garden, Ireland); 125 Ron Evans/The Garden Picture Library (Bakers House, Shrops.); 126 John Glover; 127 Clive Nichols (Green Farm Plants, Designer Piet Oudolf); 128 Jerry Harpur (East Lambrook Manor, Somerset); 129 above Andrew Lawson (East Lambrook Manor, Somerset); 129 below Steven Wooster/The Garden Picture Library (East Lambrook Manor, Somerset); 130–131 Sunniva Harte (Owner Ethne Clark); 132 left Steven Wooster (Designer Beth Chatto, Beth Chatto Gardens, Essex); 132–133 Clive Nichols (Green Farm Plants/Designer Piet Oudolf); 134 Derek St Romaine; 135 S & O Mathews (RHS Wisley, Surrey); 136 Steven Wooster (Designer Beth Chatto, Beth Chatto Gardens, Essex); 137 Jerry Pavia (Hadspen Garden and Nursery, Somerset); 138 Andrew Lawson (Designer Beth Chatto, Beth Chatto Gardens, Essex); 139 above Jerry Pavia (Longwood Garden,Penn, USA); 139 below Andrew Lawson (Designer Christopher Lloyd, Great Dixter, East Sussex); 140 Sunniva Harte; 141 Roger Foley (US Botanical Garden, Washington DC); 142–143 Sunniva Harte (Merriments Garden, East Sussex); 144 Sunniva Harte; 145 Lamontagne/The Garden Picture Library; 146 John Glover; 147 above S & O Mathews (Beth Chatto Garden, Essex); 147 below Clive Nichols (Green Farm Plants/Designer Piet Oudolf); 148 above Roger Foley (Wolfgang Oehme Garden, USA); 148 below left Derek Fell (Ton ter Linden Garden, Holland); 149 Jerry Harpur (Designer Ton ter Linden, Netherlands); 150–151 Clive Nichols (Green Farm Plants/Designer Piet Oudolf); 152 Jerry Harpur (Designers Oehme & Van Sweden, Washington DC, USA); 153 above Roger Foley (Oehme Garden/Designers Oehme & Van Sweden); 153 below Roger Foley (Designers Oehme & Van Sweden, Robinson Garden, USA); 154 above Jerry Pavia (Hadspen House, Somerset); 154 above centre Stephen Robson (West Dean College, Sussex); 154 below centre Stephen Robson (Ballymaloe Cookery School Gardens, Co. Cork, Ireland); 154 below Jerry Harpur (West Park, Munich, Germany); 155 above Steven Wooster (Designer Christopher Lloyd, Great Dixter, East Sussex) 155 above centre Jerry Harpur (Inverewe Garden, Ross & Cromarty, Highland); 155 below centre Andrew Lawson (Designer Urs Walser, Hermannshof, German); 155 below John Glover (Sticky Wicket , Dorset)

Author Acknowledgments

I would like to thank the following for their help in the making of this book: Joy Larkcom, Ethne Clarke, David Shapero, my friends on the Worldwide Web and the team at Conran Octopus.